PRACTICAL VISUALIZATION

D0562260

Also in this series

COLOUR THERAPY
Mary Anderson
HOW TO BE A MEDIUM
J. Donald Walters
HOW TO DEVELOP YOUR ESP
Zak Martin
MEDITATION: THE INNER WAY
Naomi Humphrey
UNDERSTANDING ASTRAL PROJECTION
Anthony Martin
UNDERSTANDING THE CHAKRAS
Peter Rendel
UNDERSTANDING THE I CHING
Tom Riseman
UNDERSTANDING NUMEROLOGY
D. Jason Cooper
UNDERSTANDING PALMISTRY
Mary Anderson
UNDERSTANDING REINCARNATION
J. H. Brennan
UNDERSTANDING RUNES
Michael Howard

PRACTICAL VISUALIZATION

Self-development through visualization and affirmation

by

Chris Odle

THE AQUARIAN PRESS

First published 1990

© CHRIS ODLE 1990

All rights reserved. No part of this book may be reproduced or utilized in any form or by any means, electronic or mechanical, including photocopying, recording, or by any information storage and retrieval system without permission in writing from the Publisher.

British Library Cataloguing in Publication Data

Odle, Chris
Practical visualization: self-development through
visualization and affirmation. – (Aquarian paths to inner power)
1. Self-development. Use of visualization
I. Title
158.1

ISBN: 0-85030-978-6

The Aquarian Press is part of the Thorsons Publishing Group, Wellingborough, Northamptonshire, NN8 2RQ, England

Printed in Great Britain by William Collins, Sons & Co. Ltd, Glasgow

1 3 5 7 9 10 8 6 4 2

CONTENTS

Introduction 7

1. You Create the World 17
2. Preparation/Relaxation 27
3. Dream On 33
4. Basic Visualization and Affirmation 44
5. Practical Visualizations 64
6. Advanced Techniques 103

Appendix: Modern Spells 123
Index 143

INTRODUCTION

This book is designed to be a thorough study of visualization and affirmation. These are mental processes we use all the time, often without realizing. The term visualization has come to encompass all the sensory imaginations, not just the visual: hearing a bell or smelling a rose in your mind are two examples of non-visual sensing. When we are on our way to a party and we imagine what it will be like, when we have a row with our lover and we imagine things being peaceful, when there are loads of unpaid bills and we imagine having the money to pay, when we are sad and we think about being happy, all these are visualizations.

Affirmation means 'to make firm' and this term applies to how we use words to create. For instance, when we ask someone how they are, they might reply 'I am very well' or 'I'm just surviving.' Their answer is an 'affirmation' of how they feel about their lives.

The art/science of visualization and affirmation is a conscious look at naturally existing mental and emotional behaviour — that's why it can be so powerful. At present the label 'creative visualization' is very popular and refers to utilizing the sensory imagination to help create something that we want and/or need.

7

How it works

A lot of modern and alternative psychology recognizes the importance of mental attitude in determining the experiences we have. A simple analogy may illustrate this. We could say that as individuals we are like pieces of a jigsaw puzzle, we all have a particular shape. This shape corresponds to the type of person that we are — the ideas and thoughts that we have in turn lead to the action we take. Most of us are rather inflexible, so that our piece of the jigsaw doesn't change much. It will only 'fit in' to a limited number of pictures.

We are attracted to situations that reflect who we are, often in a very conscious way. By changing our attitudes and thoughts, we automatically change the shape of the jigsaw piece. This in turn means that we will fit into different situations. Creative visualization lets us create or give birth to something new in us — to change who we are.

Thought comes first

It is important to understand how the man-made world as we know it came about. Everything we created started off as thought or impulse — if we make a cup of tea the process usually starts with the *thought* of making it, maybe in response to the feeling of thirst. Thus conscious and subconscious thoughts/feelings/impulses are of the utmost significance. They are the root of our experiences of life.

Negative and positive attitudes

All of us have many negative attitudes, they may have arisen from early conditioning, or perhaps they stem from bad reactions to later experiences. These negative patterns hold us back from growing, opening up and finding out who we are. Visualization is a very powerful way of replacing negative impulses with positive ones. In the actual process of visualizing a positive situation we start to create it, indeed to a certain extent it is already created. This is important and needs to be understood. The art/science of visualization is really very simple — it recognizes psychological processes and uses techniques to focus and channel them in certain ways.

People use a multitude of creative visualizations the whole time! For instance, take two people that know nothing about creative visualization, both going to a job interview — Mrs Negative and Mrs Positive. Mrs Negative is very apprehensive about getting the job, on the way to the interview she chews things over in her mind and imagines the worst, she feels scared and worries about what questions she will be asked. She *sees* the interview going badly. Mrs Negative has already created her experience of that interview to a certain extent.

Mrs Positive on the other hand is a lot more relaxed, she wants the job but is not too attached to getting it. She imagines the interview going well, she sees herself getting on with the people there. As an idle fantasy she imagines them shaking her hand and smiling, following on from this she pictures her joy on receiving her letter of acceptance. Mrs Positive has created a positive attitude towards the interview and this has started to create a successful interview. Thought creates experience. We all go around with negative mental tapes that we don't need.

The limits of visualization

There are a lot of grand claims made about what can be achieved through visualization. However, some of these are very misleading. For instance some quarters maintain that visualization can only be used for good — this is nonsense!

Visualization is a way of focusing human nature and as such can be used for good or bad. A murderer or bank robber may spend many hours visualizing their crime. When someone has a lot of ill thoughts towards you they don't have to tell you overtly — you can sense it from them.

Also, many people expect something for nothing. They think they can sit in their chairs, half read a couple of books and their whole lives will radically change! We are not trying to say that life should be hard work, far from it, but a lot of the success of our visualizations is dependent on choosing the right goals, knowing what is possible and being open to getting our needs met as well as our wants.

Specialist help

It is important to be realistic and honest. Although visualization and affirmation can bring about complete changes, for some these techniques may be an escape from facing themselves — they could have problems that are so deeply rooted that the only way to tackle them is to seek specialist help from a psychological expert. This book is not put forward as a universal remedy for all of life's ailments: that key lies within each one of us. Different individuals need different catalysts.

Intent or will

Our intent or will is extremely significant. It may be defined as the actual vibrations that we have and put out — our life's direction. For instance, suppose someone was unemployed and wanted a job. They might decide to do a simple visualization to get one. They imagine working and earning a lot of money. They try to open up to any new opportunities that come along. Their conscious intent seems OK. They feel as though they want to work. They try to find it etc., but whatever their conscious impulses, on a deeper subconscious level the person concerned may be extremely lazy and just want vast amounts of money for doing nothing. Or perhaps they have a strong fear of failing due to previous experiences in the past. So their truer and deeper intent/will goes against what they are consciously trying to create. As will be explained later, by knowing this we can help change our deep seated attitudes. It is very difficult to be completely honest with ourselves about what we feel and think. A lot of the time it's hard enough getting in touch with our feelings even if we want to.

Virtue and protection

Let us examine briefly the effect our intent or will has on creating certain experiences. For example, take someone whose main intent in life is to amass money regardless of how they do it. That is their aim and goal and they focus their mental energy in that way. Their drive and greed override moral considerations. Let's say they come across creative visualization and decide to use a few visualizations to attract more wealth into their life. However, their intent or focused vibration is a desire for wealth irrespective of the cost in other ways. So they are opening themselves up to money in any way possible as long as a lot of it arrives. A lot of channels for money arriving may be fine, such as winning the pools or placing a lucky bet; but others may not be, such as getting run over and receiving compensation or a relative dying and getting an inheritance.

The other side of the coin may be someone who really wanted a satisfying job *and* piles of money. Their feeling and intent was that they genuinely wanted the money only if the job was rewarding for them in other ways as well, they wanted to use their positive skills in a fashion that would benefit others. So that was their intent, their vibration, what they were asking for. With this they would definitely attract themselves into a good situation.

We get what we ask for

To a certain extent, we get what we ask for. Think about this. What do you really want?

For the good and love of all

If we say or write this down at the end of any visualizations we have, it is a statement to ourselves and the world that we are open to attracting ourselves into a situation and experience that is for the good and love of all. This will help ensure a harmonious result, all you have to do is to feel a little bit genuinely open to this, and you will create it in some way. This will be explained more fully later on.

Magic and visualization

A lot of the techniques used in modern visualization have been around for a long time. They have been dressed up in the roles of different western and eastern magical traditions, often made obtuse and inaccessible to the general public. Visualization has been used extensively in western magic, witchcraft is full of it. Visualization could easily be termed modern magic. The only real difference now is that no paraphernalia tends to be used, it is kept purely in the mind.

There has always been an aura of excitement about magic,

and so there is for anyone who starts to have visualizations. The results are never sure when we genuinely open ourselves up to the new. So little is really known about the way our minds work, and it is also a very individual thing. What is true and works for one might not for another. Visualization is very positive as it makes accessible for the first time really magical principles that until now were only available to a few. The powerful and strange truths of esoteric traditions have emerged from obscurity to become part of current thought and therapies.

Modern therapies

Modern psychotherapies, such as psychosynthesis, are now eager to use any techniques that enhance our understanding of ourselves. Freud, who founded modern analysis, started off a trend towards a very analytical 'heady' psychology although he initiated some important concepts. Free word association allowed people to gain access to their subconscious. Different psychologies have varied words and structures to describe the mind. For example, in Freudian symbolism we have the ego, the id, the conscious and the subconscious. Jungians may 'cut the cake' or divide the mind into other phrases. These structures are never totally true. Just as the description is never the same as the described, structures can be used to gain an understanding from a certain angle, but we should always see their limitations. What most modern psychological theories have in common is some sort of concept of an unconscious, a part of our brain consisting of thoughts, feelings, memories, etc., of which we are not conscious. This is both very important and very obvious. If we stop to think about and feel what we are experiencing and are aware of at any one time, we realize how unaware we really are. What we are unconscious of within ourselves comes out most visibly in dreams; however the truth is that by gradually opening up and being more 'conscious' of ourselves we can begin to see how our behaviour is often very conditioned — we react almost in a reflex way in certain situations because of our experiences in the past. It is as though we have programmed ourselves. By seeing these 'programmes' we can begin to free ourselves from their negative effects.

Modern psychotherapies use visualization techniques to help people gain access to what is not normally conscious. As well as this, visualization can help us stretch and develop our imagination and allow us to relax and play creatively in much the same way as a child.

The New Age

The New Age has come to represent the tremendous surge of interest in alternative fields over the past few years. This trend is regarded by some as part of the dawning of a new era in human consciousness, popularly termed 'The Age of Aquarius'. Astrologically this relates to the precession of the sun's equinox into the zodiac sign of Aquarius towards the end of the century.

Some of the subjects covered, such as palmistry and astrology, have a strong tradition, whilst others like affirmations and creative visualization present old concepts in a totally fresh format. What they all share is a spiritual framework that relates to life as a whole. In this, they differ from more conventional and autonomous sciences like mathematics. It is a common mistake to look at the New Age in a purely scientific and logical light. The supposed objectivity of science only represents current acceptance of subjective opinions. This objectivity is all too readily idealized and respected. History shows how inconsistent science can be.

The approach to the so-called New Age is often confusing. Although there is a lot of shared understanding and agreement, many authors have different ideas and values.

INTRODUCTION

These discrepancies are natural and creative, perhaps in much the same way that painters will evolve varied images of the same sunset.

Everyone has an individual truth and a way of expressing it; because of this it is gently suggested that you read other books as well. Evaluate carefully the information and knowledge you come across. Make your own mind up — no one else can be you — for you.

CHAPTER ONE

YOU CREATE THE WORLD

How to use this book

This book has been structured so that you can either read right through it and then work through the visualizations that you desire, or if you want to get stuck in straight away, peruse Chapter 2 and then proceed directly to Chapter 5. This fifth chapter has techniques listed under headings for every area of our lives. However it is usually far better to understand the context of our lives before we work at a visualization; it is for this reason that we suggest you look through the whole book. Sometimes just by seeing something about ourselves a block is released and there is no need for a visualization. It is the author's sincere intention that you feel free to use this book as you wish.

The importance of thought

Human consciousness really is an amazing thing. It is because of it that we have moved so far from other forms of life. The phrase 'so far' is used to indicate great movement but is in no way a judgement or observation on whether that movement is good or bad. Let us for a moment compare a human and an animal such as a squirrel. A squirrel seems almost entirely ruled by instincts, probably quite simple; these basic drives fuel its life. The need for food and shelter and procreation dictate action. Humans on the other hand have, to a certain extent, managed to free themselves from their instincts. By this we mean that as long as we have sufficient funds we can supply our basic needs. Birth control even gives us power over reproduction. Obviously a lot of people in the world are starving, and often people in such situations will spend a lot of time as the squirrel does, trying to get that basic need met.

X-factor

Humans seem to have a different sort of consciousness from other forms of life. They stand out. This X-factor would appear to be connected to some sort of self-awareness. The ability to step back, make choices, to react in a conscious way. We are a form of life that is deeply conscious of itself.

Thought and mind

How and in what form we think is strongly connected to this X-factor of self-awareness. In most civilizations language is passed on and taught to a newly born baby, thus our first experiences of being conscious and being alive are strongly linked to language. So our minds become conditioned to think in words, that is the way we have been shown. Often when we have to make a decision we will talk things over internally or sometimes think out loud. This may seem terribly obvious and of no consequence, but when we are born we do not have any of this. To a certain extent we are like a blank page and our early experiences start to create who we will become. Thought and mind become very joined, and many people then identify who they are far too much with their thoughts.

Repression and the subconscious

Why do we decide to do the things we do? How much freedom do we actually have? It is so hard to see the full importance of our conditioning. Let us take a simple example to illustrate this. A young girl was repeatedly told at an early age by her teacher that she was no good and would never be able to pass her exams because she was stupid. That girl reacted at the time by believing what the teacher was saying and so stopped attempting to work hard and pass her exams. Someone else may well have reacted in a different way thinking, 'I'll show that teacher,' which shows that we can react differently to a negative stimulus. We do have a choice. However the girl reacted in a negative way, she took on board what the teacher was saying. She conditioned herself. Now, later on in life, she will still have that belief because she created it along with the teacher, many years ago. That belief will probably be repressed because it is too painful to have it conscious, and if it is conscious and she can't deal with it she will block it out. It may arise in certain situations in her life and she might sort it out; for example, when she is a lot older she may decide to do an Open University course, or that negative belief might prevent her from ever studying again. It is not necessary that she should study, just that it would be good for her to be free to choose.

Patterns and identity

So all of us carry around with us loads and loads of conditioning, patterns of behaviour; some good, some bad. These patterns have a profound effect on our lives. Although many patterns are very bad for us, we are very reluctant to change them. Much of this is due to the basic human problem of identity. This, in turn, relates to our experience of being alive, our self-consciousness. Most people have hardly any idea of *who* they are. *Who* we are, *what* we are cannot really be put into words, it is something that is constantly moving and changing. Because most people are fundamentally afraid of this on a very deep level, they love to categorize and label life and themselves. What we are cannot be known because, to know something is to have an image or structure of it, and not to experience it directly. This may seem confusing, but I am not trying to be obtuse, just to get to the root of some important concepts.

The mind loves to know. That is what we are taught and conditioned to think from the start. The relevance of this to our lives now is enormous. Even if we have very self-destructive patterns of behaviour we may find it very difficult to change them, even if we have a strong desire to do so. Why should this be? Much of it is fear of the unknown, because of our insecurities we often cling to identities that are bad for us. By identities I mean who we are, our life. As an example, take a drug addict — almost the extreme of what a negative pattern can be. A bad heroin addict will do almost anything to make sure that they get more of the drug. By this stage they do not even enjoy the effects of it, it is just relief from the symptoms of not having it. They try to stop but they do not *know* how to. They are unable to find a happy way of living without it and so even though it is such a painful way of being alive they go back to it. To a certain extent it is comforting because it is something that is known and so has a certain value as an identity — something to be. We could compare this to a

20

couple in a negative relationship — they split up but get back together as this is preferable to separating, the getting back together is a relief from the pain of separation.

We create the world

Most people are unaware of just how much influence they have on life itself. We are all centres of consciousness, and society is made up of people like you and me. We all project our feelings of powerlessness onto convenient hooks such as the government, and think if only they passed this law or that one our lives would be different. The reality is that this is just one aspect. We have a tremendous part to play, what we think, feel and do has a direct effect on the world. The best way to change things is from the inside. We *create* the world, we evolve with it. Because of the way in which our minds have evolved, by understanding and changing our thoughts we can directly influence our experience of life. We have that choice. Creative visualization can provide powerful techniques to help us do this.

Creative visualization and change

A small change in our attitude can lead to profound changes in our lives. Take for example someone who is extremely shy and finds it very hard to socialize. They usually turn down all social invitations, although this is based on the fear of meeting people, rather than a genuine desire to be alone. They make a decision to accept the next three invites or opportunities they get. That difference in attitude could easily alter their whole life. That one small change. An interesting point is that breaking away and moving on from patterns nearly always involves a step into the unknown.

Creative visualization immediately changes us in some way. When we have changed our thoughts and focused them, we start to create something. This is important, the change is created by the fact that we do it. This in itself may lead to some sort of result. Change exists in the present.

One of the best things about creative visualization is that even if we are in conflict about something and have fears and doubts about doing it, the mere fact that we take a few minutes to visualize it happening in a positive way is a statement to ourselves that we are open to it. It's like planting a seed which will germinate as long as we have enough positive soil.

Choosing our reality

With creative visualization we can choose to try to change our lives in anyway that we want. To a large extent what we really desire on a deep conscious and subconscious level is what we attract into our lives. All of us attract a huge range of vibrations into our lives. Focusing our energies through visualizations helps us to attract the things that we want and need and more importantly find out what we do desire. That's enough words for now. Let's look at a few basic visualizations and exercises. First of all, just to open up a bit, sit down with two pieces of paper and a pen.

Write it out — love/hate

This is a very simple exercise that helps us to see how we feel and think about our lives.

Take the first piece of paper and write down all the things you dislike about your life, personally and generally. There will probably be a few that spring to mind quite readily. When you have exhausted these take a few extra moments to reflect and see if you can find others that aren't quite so obvious. Stop when you feel like it. When you have finished read through the list a couple of times and digest what you have written. Throw away this list if you wish.

Next, take the other piece of paper and this time write out all the things you like about your life, once again both personally and generally. Take some extra time to find some things that aren't initially that obvious. When finished, read through it as before. Keep this list if you wish.

Writing things out is often a good way of clearing out and focusing our minds. It is the start of making the internal, external. When we are confused about something and our thoughts go round and round some simple writing will often put it in perspective. A good example of this is if we know we have a lot of different things to do one day; if we keep trying to list them internally it can be very hard, however, writing a list clarifies it immediately.

Writing it also a good way of getting in touch with our deeper feelings, beginning to penetrate the subconscious, to make conscious what is unconscious. That is why it is suggested that you take a few moments longer after putting down the thoughts that come straight away. This is when feelings and impulses from deeper levels start to emerge.

Basic visualization

Now for some visualizations proper. These need hardly any preparation. The first time just sit or lie in a position you feel comfortable with. Have your eyes open or shut, whichever you prefer.

What you want/what you need

First of all just be still and let your mind settle, now think about all the things that you want in your life. They could be anything at all, don't hold back — give your imagination free rein. Your thoughts may change really quickly but that doesn't matter. You might want to improve some already existing situations or you might want to change those situations completely. Look at all the areas of your life that you want to.

After a while try to pinpoint the one area that you would most like to change, the one that is the most unsatisfactory at the moment. When you have done this imagine how you would like it to change, try to see in your mind's eye an image of how you would like it to be. Believe that it will actually occur. When you have finished — and this is entirely up to you — it could be 30 seconds or 2 hours, if you have the energy start to explore what you need. If you're a bit tired by now leave this until another time.

When you explore what your needs are, think and feel about whether your needs are being met. As before, focus at the end on one particular need you feel is not being met as well as you would like. Visualize the change that you want.

These combined exercises show us how we feel about what we want and what we need, as well as allowing us to see how we feel about life as it is for us at present. Sometimes it's far easier to locate what we want as opposed to what we need. Getting in touch with our needs can be very hard.

How we visualize

It is important to clear up any possible confusion about what it is like to actually visualize. Many people see in their mind's eye. They have images and pictures of things — most people do this. So if, for example, they were doing the needs/wants exercise they would have pictures of life as they might want it. Thus vision is one of the most common sensory experiences internally. But we can also *sense* sounds, tastes, smells, textures. Some find it difficult to sense any of these internally, that's OK if you are like that, just think in thoughts to yourself. Visualization is just a blanket term and really represents the whole range of internal sensing. However, it is most strongly related to sight, and sight for most people who visualize is the most common internal sense; because of this a lot of visualizations make full use of our internal sense of vision.

People who find this difficult and/or tend to think solely in words, will find affirmations much more constructive as these just use simple verbal statements.

Affirmations

A lot of people find that affirmations are a very powerful way to bring about quick changes. An affirmation is a way of 'making firm'. They can be written or spoken. A basic example could be:

'I now attract lots of money into my life.'

As a simple introduction to affirmations, write out a list of up to five affirmations along the lines of the example. Choose situations, people or things that you want to attract into your life:

i.e. 'I now attract ... into my life.'

Don't worry if you can only think of a couple, that's fine. What's important is that you have a genuine desire to receive what you have asked for. When you have written them down, say them quietly to yourself internally and then speak them out loud. There are quite a lot of different ways to construct affirmations and these will be discussed in more detail later on.

These last two exercises are the basis of visualization and affirmation. It really is as simple as that. If we want to effect certain changes in our lives and we have an idea of what we want, we start to create it on an inner level.

So, the basic principles are very simple:

1. Decide what you want to create, what your will or intent is. This is termed 'setting your goal'.

2.   Give your intent/will a form. With visualization this is usually a visual image, with affirmation it's linguistic — we put into words what we want to make firm.

With both visualization and affirmation we increase the charge or current of our form by repeatedly creating it as strongly as we can. Everything starts off as a creative impulse, but not all creative impulses mature, which is why it is good to understand the overall context of ourselves and the world, so we can choose realities and goals which are positive, healthy and natural for us. When we try to be ourselves the world opens out beautifully. Hopefully this book will help that happen in your life.

CHAPTER TWO

PREPARATION/ RELAXATION

People are often a bit confused when they first start to do visualizations as to the best state of mind to be in. Many books stress the importance of being relaxed. It is now widely thought that the brain produces different kinds of waves or vibrations, and when we are in a state of deep relaxation the sorts of rhythms we create are very conducive to successful visualization.

This seems to be true in many cases and has relevance to many states of self-hypnosis, there is no doubt that a deeply relaxed mind will accept hypnotic suggestions much more readily than an alert mind. In many ways certain visualization methods are self-hypnotic — we are trying to re-programme ourselves. However, it would be a grave mistake to assume that, for visualizations to work, we have to be in a deep state of relaxation.

The truth is that visualizations can be done in almost any situation. For example when we are doing physical exercise or even just walking down the street, the fact that our bodies are creating some sort of rhythm seems to distract the mind a little and so allows us to focus more easily. We could say that a meditative state of mind is positive for undertaking visualizations. That meditative state could be passive as in deep relaxation, or active as in jogging or walking. Having said this does not mean that non-meditative states don't work — often by idle day-dreaming we can create profound changes or gain strong insights into the undercurrents of our minds.

The fact is that different things work best for different people. In India they have a saying 'no five fingers the same' and this really does apply to the world of visualization. What follows in the next few pages are different techniques to help you relax. Choose the ones that you feel comfortable with. If none of them suit you relax in the way that you know best and are happy with.

The visualizations that are given in the rest of the book will just have 'relax' written at the beginning if it is appropriate to be in a relaxed state of mind. If the particular visualization is suited to other conditions, details will be laid out. Please feel free to experiment, there are no hard and fast rules, you will only find out what works for you by trying different things out. For instance two people doing the same visualization may discover that for one of them it only produces results if they lie on their bed for half an hour first, and do a lot of deep breathing, whilst the other has to be jogging around the block to succeed. A final point worth mentioning is that just doing a visualization will often have a very calming effect and will naturally allow you to find your own inner level.

Relaxation exercises

At first when you start doing visualization it's often enough just to sit in a chair quietly, and compose yourself. It seems to be better if you have your back straight, as in the long run this is much less tiring.

Similar to this in simplicity is lying down on a bed or something else suitable. It would be totally feasible to complete all visualizations using the above two positions.

Deep breathing

Assume one of the two postures above. Breathing is a very basic function that most of us take for granted and hardly ever stop to think about. Many people breathe using mainly the chest. Deep breathing using the abdominal muscles to inhale has a very restful and calming influence. Try inhaling air by expanding your abdominal muscles and then drawing the air up into your chest cavity. At first breathe quite slowly — intake the air for a few seconds, hold it for a couple and exhale fairly slowly. Try to breathe in and out using your nose to inhale and your mouth to exhale.

This simple procedure is the basis of deep or diaphragm breathing. If you try it you will find that in quite a short time you begin to feel the positive effects. A few minutes is quite enough to prepare you before you attempt a visualization.

Yogic techniques have developed deep breathing into a fine art and many other meditational schools make full use of it. At first just breathe at a pace that feels comfortable. This should really be enough, however if you feel you want to extend this breathing method try the following.

Further deep breathing

The main way is to use a rhythmical cycle to dictate how long you inhale, hold, and then exhale. You could start off with something fairly simple such as inhaling for three seconds, holding for three seconds, then exhaling for three seconds. Instead of watching a clock to time yourself just count internally to yourself. Now we can see how this method is useful for meditation, because we have a structure the mind is absorbed in (focusing on the breathing cycle), this focus clears the mind and allows other processes to start. Deep breathing also has an accepted effect on the nervous system and really does help one relax.

Many yogic pathways suggest that you build up the breathing cycle to quite long periods. It is advised that 10 seconds for each part of the inhalation, holding and exhalation is quite enough. It should be noted that drawing the air up into the chest and holding is important as it helps the fresh air circulate and clear out the old.

Once you have discovered the joys of deep breathing you can carry on doing it throughout your life; it's much healthier to breathe in this way. But be sensible, be guided by what feels natural: you're obviously not going to want to hold your breath for ten seconds whilst walking down the street. Try to breathe naturally. If it doesn't feel comfortable and good then it's probably not right. One further point is that if you're feeling nervous, a spot of deep breathing will greatly help you to calm down.

Total body relaxation

This is a very good exercise to do last thing at night or first thing in the morning. These two times are also very good for visualization as the mind is often extremely receptive then. So, the principle is to tense and then relax all the muscles in your body. Lie down. Start out by stretching your toes and wriggling them around; after tensing them relax totally, feel them mentally and sense how relaxed they are. Now start to work your way up your body slowly, tensing your muscles and then feeling how relaxed they are. Once you have reached your torso do your hands and arms, stretch them out, some muscles you may not be able to tense in the position you are in. Don't worry, just do what you can. When you get to your face you can relax your mouth and then finish with your eyes and scalp. Take as long as you want, but as a guideline 5-15 minutes should be ample to do your whole body. You can combine this with deep breathing if you wish.

Cat stretch

Once again this is done whilst lying down and is very good just after you wake up. Basically it's very simple, just stretch, arch your back, clasp your hands, whatever feels good. If you want some inspiration, watch a cat let go and have a good stretch — it's amazing how relaxed they look.

Candle meditation

Sit in a comfortable position and light a candle, any candle will do. Just observe the flame, try to get your mind absorbed into the shape and colour of the light. At first you may find it very hard to keep your mind concentrated on the flame as your thoughts dart all over the place. Don't worry, just bring your attention back to the flame and watch it move. This is a very good exercise to do as the mind loves rituals and is easily conditioned, so if you persevere with this exercise after a while the mere lighting of the candle will start to produce a relaxed, yet alert state of mind. You can always keep the candle alight when you start to work through a visualization. Once again, there is no time limit, watching a candle flame is a powerful meditation in itself, 5-15 minutes should be enough, though if it feels good and positive, do it for longer if you want.

Blue paper

Colours have a powerful effect on the mind, and blue has been found to have a very calming influence, particularly a deep blue. Obtain a piece of deep blue paper, place it in front of you whilst you are sitting up, and look at it. Try to sense the vibrations and feel your mind relaxing.

Everyone is an individual and so you might have a different colour that you find is very restful for you. If this is the case, get a piece of paper in that colour instead.

Personal techniques

Many people already use rituals to help them relax. These vary and could be anything from having a bath, to doing the cleaning or going for a walk. Whatever works for you is right for you.

CHAPTER THREE

DREAM ON

In this chapter we start by looking at some exercises to help us develop our imagination and to get in touch with our internal senses. Children have a natural ability to play in a very unself-conscious way. At first their imagination is pretty unlimited, they do not worry about what is possible. As we get older we start to be more and more realistic, we stop being silly. For most, thought becomes less and less imaginative and more and more restricted. Playing is essentially very creative; do you remember when you were younger how hours and hours would go by when you were absorbed in a game with friends or just playing by yourself? One of the few 'adult' pastimes that has or can have that playful creativity is sex.

It's interesting to note that a lot of businesses now have courses or pay for executives to do activities such as go-karting, or even playing at being kids again to the extent of dressing up in kids' clothes and jumping around in playpens! It's obvious that these services meet a need to redress some sort of imbalance that is caused by being a stressed-out executive. Most of us do not play enough in our lives. After examining ways in which to open up our inner creativity we will start to do visualizations proper, looking at what we actually want to create in our lives, trying to make sure that we set goals that are both realistic and good for us.

The exercises and techniques given should be regarded as starting points. If you feel like changing them, then do so. Many people when they read a book take everything on board as gospel truth, as being the only way to do something, but it is intended that the methods given here simply illustrate all the basic principles necessary for visualization, and once these principles are understood it's very easy to start creating your own systems.

Do what you enjoy

A very important point is that if doing an exercise feels like hard work it's much more difficult to do it and get a lot from it. If, on the other hand, it's really enjoyable, there is no resistance and you will actually want to do it as it's a pleasurable experience. So as regards developing our internal senses, imagine tasting, touching, hearing, seeing, smelling things that are pleasurable to you, obviously this will vary from person to person, you know best what you enjoy, so recreate that experience internally.

Senses

Touch

Relax. Touch is a sense that is often not used enough. One way to rapidly develop our sense of touch is to sit down and look around the room. Imagine touching an object, for example a chair. Sense what the texture would feel like if you ran your fingers over it, feel the material. Now move on to something else — the wall, the table, whatever else is in the room. The most important thing is to try and sense the different textures of the materials. You can do this exercise anywhere, on a bus or train for example, just look around you and imagine touching what you see.

Smell and taste

Relax. Think of what you had for your last meal. Imagine tasting it again, really try to feel as though the food is actually in your mouth, chew it.

Now imagine you were going to your favourite restaurant and you have an unlimited amount of money. Decide what you are going to order. Sense what all the food tastes like. Smell all the different aromas. If you find this a bit difficult, get some cookery books with lots of colour pictures. That extra stimulus of a large picture of some food should make it a lot easier for you to visualize yourself eating it and tasting and smelling.

As smell is such a rarely used sense compared to the others, try this additional exercise: write out a list of five smells that you really like and five that you hate; one by one sense the different smells.

Hearing

Relax. Think of your favourite musical instrument, imagine it being played. It could be classical or pop or whatever, it's up to you. Hear the sound internally. After a little practice it's very easy to hear sounds inside your head, and a lot of people listen to little snatches of music as they walk down the street.

Try listening to your favourite song, hear all the different instruments. Sometimes you can pick out all the various noises and melodies.

Another good exercise is to imagine listening to your friends. Try to hear their voices — one at a time is best. You can even have imaginary conversations.

Sight

Relax. Look at the palm of your hand for a minute or so, then close your eyes. Try to picture your palm in your mind's eye. This may be very difficult at first, but don't worry. After a few seconds (10-20) open your eyes again and look at your palm. Carry on in this way, observing your palm as it is then closing your eyes to try and build a mental picture of it. After a while and maybe some sessions you will be able to close your eyes for quite a long time and have a reasonable image of your hand. Obviously you could use anything for this exercise — flowers are good.

Another more simple exercise is to relax and shut your eyes, now imagine you are in your favourite department store, and *see* all the different goods.

Opening up

Many of us are very blocked up from childhood. We have strong inhibitions about expressing how we really feel. We are taught to be sophisticated and tidy in our manner. This exercise is designed to help us begin to relax some blocks and allow our subconscious to push through.

You will need some paper and some pens and pencils. Relax. Take a pen and hold it in the hand you use normally. Scribble on the paper, don't worry about what it will look like, just put the pen on the paper and move it around in any way that you like. Do not try to draw anything, don't think about what you are producing, just do it — move it fast or slow, try to let go and open up. When you have finished, repeat using the other hand. This scribbling is often a very good way to release inner tension.

When you have managed to scribble without worrying about the result, you can try this addition. Take another sheet of paper and, holding the pen in your main hand, draw a circle or oval with one sweeping movement of your hand and arm. Once again try not to think about it too much. Draw more circles or ovals in the same way. As before try using your other hand. You will probably be surprised as to how good these simple exercises make you feel. It's important to use both hands as we release a lot by doing this. You can always draw different shapes.

Being child-like

There is often confusion about the positive and negative attributes connected with children. There are a lot of good things about being child-like, and a lot of bad things about being childish. Look at your own life and see how much room you give yourself to play — what activities do you do which give you that sense of creativity. That's why drawing and painting are often very good ways to get back in touch with your own inner creativity. Feed your need to play — try to play regularly and do things that give you joy.

Children often have a beautiful innocence and faith in life, their eyes are wonderfully open and accepting. Some people think children are incredibly spiritual and that we should rediscover that state of child-like spirituality, however this is not the case. There are qualities that a child has that are very pure and spiritual, but in reality many kids are selfish and cruel; anyone who has children or has worked in a nursery or school will see this. Human nature is not all good, much of it is related to survival and as such drives us in certain directions. However, a child-like faith and openness is essential to visualization. Once again it's related to being open to the unknown, for although we may have a clear idea of what we want and what is good for us, we may be way off the mark. Having an open mind and heart can help us create new directions in our life — for all true creations are new.

Day-dreaming

Day-dreaming can be very instructive in showing us what areas of our lives are unfulfilled as well as giving us directions to follow and signs and symbols, about how we feel generally about what is going on.

Day-dreaming can also be done in most situations (though obviously not when concentration is required such as driving a car). Start off by choosing a fantasy about your career; maybe you wanted to be a pop star or a famous actress. If, for example, you fancied being a famous singer, you could imagine being on stage with thousands of people watching you, dream about the applause and see yourself belting out hit songs to a delirious audience. Your personal fantasy may well be something a lot quieter, for example perhaps you want to be an extremely skilled craftsman. If this is the case you could imagine making all the things you wanted to.

There are no limits to what you can day-dream about. How about visualizing your ideal partner or lover? Many people day-dream and fantasize regularly. Some of these day-dreams have strong symbolic meaning much in the same way as nocturnal dreams do. When we let go and allow our minds to wander, messages from our subconscious mind often filter through. As an example of this, it's interesting to relate how some people when they have finished a relationship have dreams or day-dream about going to their ex's funeral, or just that their ex has died. This initially may seem a bit morbid, but when you examine the symbolism it becomes apparent that death in this case signifies a psychological process of letting go, something that was there is there no longer. So watch your idle fantasies and see if they are trying to tell you something.

Pathworking

Pathworking and guided imagery are very good ways to open

up our minds and imagination. A pathworking is a story, a journey that is written down with a simple structure that allows our minds to explore and receive different images.

Three different voyages are given here. One of the best ways to use them is to record them slowly on tape, then relax — lying down is often good — and play the pathworking back. Another method people use is to take it in turns to read it to each other, or have a group and one person leads. What's interesting about doing a pathworking with two or more, is comparing the symbols and pictures that you experience. It's amazing how often people share symbolism.

The three stories given here have been specifically designed so that you can use them time and time again and still discover and create new feelings and thoughts. Most people find it easier to visualize with their eyes closed. Once you have tried them, why not write one of your own, there are no barriers as to what you could create, and it's very much like being a child again where boundaries to what is and what isn't possible do not exist.

If you have not got a tape recorder or don't have someone else to do them with, they still work very well if you read a couple of lines, visualize and then read some more. Try to use as many internal senses as possible. Most of us just use vision and sound. Often it helps to jot down details of interesting images that you get, for they may relate to the future or give you symbolic or literal knowledge about your life.

The sea

We start off with a simple pathworking to help you use your imagination and stretch your internal sensing. At first while you visualize, close your eyes.

Relax. You are by the sea on a golden beach. It is deserted. Walk up to the edge of the lapping waves and look around. Smell the air and listen to the gentle sea as it lightly cascades on the sand. Take your shoes and socks off if you feel like it.

Suddenly you notice a large shell at your feet, you pick it up. You put it to your ear and hear a subtle sea sound, it seems to whisper something to you. What does it say? Replacing the shell you walk up the beach towards a cove. Birds fly overhead and you hear them cry out.

You walk up to the cove and go in, it's very dark and slightly cold, it feels a bit cramped and seems to extend into a small tunnel. The wind starts to blow in and across your face. Look around and see what you can make out in the dim light.

You sit by a little rock pool and look down, amongst the anemones and seaweed is a whole jumble of objects, you reach down and pull one out. You examine it and may decide to take it back with you.

Walking back out of the cove you make your way towards the sea again. You look around and take in the scenery, you notice some lovely hills in the distance. More birds fly across the brilliant sun and clear blue sky.

You lie down a few feet from the waves, close your eyes and feel the warm heat from the sun. Your whole body feels aglow and you lie there basking for a few minutes. Listen to the waves, the birds. You lie there with your eyes shut, totally relaxed.

Open your eyes to end your pathworking. Relax for a couple of minutes before getting up. You can repeat this sea visualization as many times as you want, try to use as many different senses as possible. Be creative, you don't have to stick to the directions strictly! If you feel like it, pick up handfuls of sand and throw them around. The pathworking is just a guideline, do what you want on the beach by the sea, you could swim or run or spend the whole time lying down. It's up to you.

The forest

And now for something a bit more imaginative — here you will have to work/play a bit harder!

Relax. You are in the middle of a lovely forest, there is light but you aren't sure what time it is. You are on a path, flanked by trees, that winds up a hill. Stop and look around, notice what the trees look like, hear birds singing. Walk up to a tree and touch it to feel its bark.

On one side as you walk on is an astonishing collection of flowers, all shapes and colours, stop and smell them, look at the colours, stroke the delicate petals. An animal leaps across your path, you watch it as it darts off into the foliage.

You carry on through the forest and come across a small hut with a door. It is marked 'the past'. Slowly you open it and go in. The hut is full of objects that all have happy associations from your past, you walk in and close the door. All around you on shelves and on the floor are items and objects connected with happy experiences you have had. Pick some up and remember. Stay in the hut for as long as you want. When you leave you walk back down the path. Look, listen, touch, smell.

As you approach your starting point you notice with surprise a table set for two. A good friend of yours then appears with a hamper. You greet each other and sit down to eat the meal they have brought. The atmosphere is light and positive as you sit chatting. You feel very warm. You say to your friend exactly what you want to, if there is anything you've wanted to mention, to get off your chest, say it now. Express yourself freely and enjoy yourself.

When you have finished eating and talking you stand up and turn around to stretch. When you look back your friend and the table and chairs have gone. Stand there for a moment feeling happy and satisfied.

Open your eyes. Relax for a couple of minutes. The next time you do the visualization you can try changing it a bit. The hut could have absolutely anything inside. Just imagine a sign on it saying what is there. For example it could say 'the future' and this time when you go in there may be objects, people or pictures related to the future. Don't be afraid to experiment.

Space travel

Now a really simple pathworking designed to really stretch your mind.

Relax. You are in a spaceship, strapped in and about to take off. Look around you and see the controls. You reach out and press the start button. The engines start up and you feel the tremendous build up of energy. Slowly the spaceship starts to move up, you look out of the window as the ground gets further and further away. Faster and faster you accelerate, piercing the sky and clouds, you finally leave earth, you look back as the spaceship slows down. You wonder where it is taking you.

The rest is up to you. You can take your space craft anywhere you want, just visualize some simple controls and go travelling. You can visit any planets or stars that you want, you could land and explore a strange world. Maybe there would be air on it that you could breathe, or perhaps you have to wear a space suit. Are there aliens there? What is the scenery like?

Once you have finished exploring, visualize your ship travelling back to earth, then slowly descending to near where you started. To finish open your eyes and sit quietly for a few moments.

This last pathworking is mainly created by you. You can see how easy it is, so now you could write your own little stories and record them or read them out. Try to devise scenarios that are enjoyable.

Passion

Some people really like doing pathworkings whilst others don't at all. There is little point forcing yourself to do something you hate. It would be far better to find exercises and visualizations that you feel excited about. Excitement is a very powerful energy — it's full of life.

Life and passion are so important. How many things in your life do you feel passionately about? What really turns you on? When we do something with a passion there is no resistance, it's as though life energy flows through us. We are being true in some way to who we are. A lot of things that people do with a passion are very destructive, yet that same passionate energy can be so totally constructive. What makes you feel alive?

CHAPTER FOUR

BASIC VISUALIZATION AND AFFIRMATION

Now that we have stretched and developed our imaginative faculties, let's start doing some practical visualizations. The basic principle could not be more simple: what we want to occur we visualize. That's it. All we are doing is focusing and structuring on an inner level. We start to create what we want. As an example let's say that we want to sort out our career. The initial problem with any visualization is to decide the goal, the aim — what we are actually trying to create.

Setting goals

There are basically two ways to set goals. One is when we have a clear image of what we want. Relating this to our career aims we may know that we want a particular job, for instance, running a fish and chip shop. Our aim may be very specific, i.e. we have seen a fish and chip premises we desire to move into, or it may be general — we just know we want to manage any suitable chippie.

However, we are often unclear about our aims. We are

dissatisfied with our current employment and seek something better, but we do not know exactly what it is that we desire. We have an image of the goal we want but it is not as clear and detailed as the above example.

Visualizing a specific goal

It's really very straightforward. Relax. Visualize yourself in the situation you wish to create. Going back to our example, you could imagine yourself walking around the shop serving customers and frying up the food. Try to use as many internal senses as possible. If you have a specific shop in mind you might go along there first and make mental notes of what it looks like inside. If not, just visualize the type of place you would like to have. Remember, to a large extent you get what you ask for. It is important that when you visualize you feel as though you are already in that situation, don't see it in the future, see it in the present. The present is all that exists.

Visualizing a symbolic goal

It is not quite as easy in this case as we do not have a definite image of what we want; all we know is that we desire a better, richer, more satisfying job.

In a sense you do have a clear goal, a different job, but we have to charge this drive, this desire, and to do that we need some sort of mental image to help our subconscious to create it in the outer world. Because of this we need to symbolize our desire in some way. The symbol will be our link to our deep mind. Taking our career example, what could symbolize us having a new job? It could be anything, for instance you could visualize yourself talking to a friend and they say, 'I hear you've got a really good new job.' You could sense how satisfying it feels to be in gainful employment. Feel it as though it is already true. A proper symbol would be something like seeing yourself sitting on the top of a ladder feeling happy, the ladder is a symbol that represents 'getting to the top' in some way.

Symbols are very interesting: some are universal and nearly everyone will relate to them, others are much more individual. To symbolize getting a new job you could picture yourself with all the things having a new job would represent to you. Remember — symbols give your will or intent, form.

Suppose we wanted to attract happiness into our lives. We could imagine ourselves feeling happy with birds singing and symbolic hearts around us. The heart is a well-known symbol of love and happiness.

Specific versus symbolic

People sometimes get confused about what sort of goal to set to resolve a particular situation. It's important to realize that on one level we don't know very much about how our minds work, it's a very nebulous field. Because of this it's good to experiment. Suppose we needed £2,000, we could visualize ourselves holding exactly £2,000 cash or we could visualize lots of money bags. The money bags would be symbolic and the £2,000 specific. Try both and see which works best for you.

There are no hard and fast rules, this is what a lot of people find difficult to understand. They want everything laid out in black and white. Chapter 5 was specifically created so that anyone who wants to change a certain area of their life can quickly locate three or four practical visualizations to help them. But after doing some visualizations you will find it much easier to evolve your own, as you will have gained understanding from experience.

Be open

It does not matter that you are unsure of what goal you want or how it will come about. When you visualize be open to receiving what is best for you; trust and all will be well. Remember, if you are uncertain about the possible outcome, use a universal affirmation.

Universal affirmations

When we try to achieve a certain goal there are different ways this goal may be created. For instance, suppose we are trying to get a new car. Our desire may be for a new car at any cost and we do not care how this result comes about. There are obviously many different 'channels'. For example, a friend of ours may die in a car crash and his family offer us his car, or someone we know dies of a serious disease and we once again receive their vehicle. If our motives are pure, then we won't create unpleasantness. Life is a strange thing and it's not always easy to judge what is good and what is bad. The energy we put out is the energy we create with. Often, even though our conscious intent is sound, on a deeper subconscious level we are mixed up and confused.

The way a lot of people pursue money for its own sake is a good example of how universal affirmations can prevent us from attracting situations where we get what we want (our goal) but not in the way that we want. Even if we have mixed motives about achieving a certain goal, by using a universal affirmation we protect ourselves and others. It is a statement to the world and to ourselves that although we may be unsure about what we are doing, we only want to create something that is positive. One friend of mine uses 'for the good and love of all'. All you do is to say it or write it, it's a protective measure to ensure that whatever results from your endeavours will have a positive effect. Shakti Gawain in her book *Creative Visualisation* suggests: 'This, or something better, now manifests for me in totally satisfying and harmonious ways for the highest good of all concerned.'

Either of these two universal affirmations are excellent for practical use. If you feel unsure about the possible outcome of a visualization it is advised that you use a universal affirmation — it's a statement to yourself and the world that you only want a positive outcome. However, it must be said that words are words and do not necessarily reflect our true intent. It is our intent and the vibration of it that will decide what happens. Sincerity and virtue truly protect us.

Affirmations

Affirmations are very powerful and easy to create, and add a lot of energy to any visualization you undertake. Basically we use words to make an affirmation of what we want. It is very important to be as positive as possible. Create positivity as opposed to getting rid of negativity. For example, suppose we feel that we get angry far too much, the way to construct a positive affirmation would be along the lines of:

'I now feel peaceful and serene all the time', or
'Peace and serenity flow into my life.'

Do not create an affirmation like:

'I now feel less angry' or 'I now feel no anger.'

You may wonder why the two different ways should have such a polarized effect; this is because of what they focus on. In the first examples we tune into positive energy, in the second negative.

Think about the difference between feeling 'peaceful and

serene' and 'not feeling angry'. Which would you rather create in your life. So remember to always focus on the positive and the new, this is very important; we are trying to be creative and creativity is always new, fresh, a birth. The energy of the new will push out the old. Do not focus on the old, for if you do it is much more likely to breed conflict. Conflicts are never resolved on or at the same level at which they exist. The resolution moves things on, we grow.

To give you some ideas about how to make up your own affirmations, here are some examples for a few different areas of our lives. Language is a very personal thing and it's often the case that our own subconscious minds will respond best to affirmations that we ourselves have evolved.

General

'My life is totally satisfying and enjoyable in every way.'
'I am totally open to all that is positive.'
'Life gets better and better all the time.'
'Love and energy pour into my life.'

Money

'I have plenty of money.'
'For all that I want and need, the money is there.'
'I am open to receiving an abundance of wealth.'

Love

'I am full of love.'
'I have a beautiful loving relationship.'
'My relationship with ... gets better all the time.'
'I have a wonderful passionate bond with ... .'
'I attract the most positive partner possible.'

Work

'I'm so happy at work.'
'Work is totally fulfilling.'

As with visualization, our aims may sometimes be very specific and sometimes not. Take, for example, relationships. We could already be in a relationship and want to improve it in a particular way, say sexually:

'My sexual relationship with ... improves rapidly.'
'I now have an incredibly satisfying sexual relationship with ... .'

Or we may be single and want to start a relationship with someone. We might have a certain person in mind:

'I now attract a loving healthy relationship with ... .'

If we don't have our eyes on anyone we could affirm:

'I now magnetize my perfect partner into my life.'

Empowering affirmations

Basically all we have to do is to put into words what we want. However, to create an affirmation that is highly charged, use words that are intense and magnetic, words that feel and mean a lot to you.

How to use affirmations

Affirmations can be spoken out loud, written, or said internally to ourselves. Try all three and see which you feel most comfortable with. It is powerful to use them all anyway. As with visualizations it's often good to be in a relaxed state of mind when we affirm. However, affirmations have the added advantage that they can be used easily at many times, due to the fact that in some situations it can take a bit of concentration to build up a mental image, but it's very easy to say a few words to yourself internally. For instance, walking to the bus stop we could affirm, 'Today I feel happy and experience amazing things.' Be creative.

Affirmations and visualizations

As well as being effective separately, these work powerfully together. It is always possible to add an affirmation at the end of a visualization (or the beginning). For instance, harping back to the chip shop, you could see yourself standing inside with the keys to the premises, say internally to yourself:

'I now own the chip shop that I've always wanted.'

Or suppose you needed to raise a bit of cash to pay for it you could affirm:

'I now have more than enough money to buy this shop,'

or

'I have bought this shop.'

Present or future

Most authorities on visualization and affirmations maintain that we should do both in the present tense, as though what we were thinking about already exists. This is undoubtedly the best way for the majority of cases. In some instances it may be creative to put our aims in the future, for instance if we have a job interview on a particular date, (say three days away) we could affirm:

'In three days' time I am accepted for ... etc.'

The next day we could affirm:

'In two days' time ... etc.'

Then finally:

'Tomorrow I am taken on by ... etc.'

Thus, we would be continually building to a particular point in time. We should never forget that the mind is not understood that well — don't be afraid to experiment and see what works for you.

How to use visualizations and affirmations as an on-going process

When we first come across the world of visualization and affirmation it can be very exciting as we work out all the changes we are going to make in our lives. It gives us a tremendous sense of what life could be. However, it's important to try and develop our lives in a way which is flowing and healthy. Often the best visualizations we do are for goals that are totally right for us, but we have been a bit blocked about obtaining them. The visualizations and affirmations unblock us and allow us to be who we are.

At first set goals that are attainable. We are not saying that you shouldn't dream and reach for the stars, just that if you want to really open your life up, it's good to do it in a natural way.

Flowing

Sometimes we set a goal which we really feel is right and we will have a strong desire to reach it. However, life doesn't agree and we feel as though we are banging our head against a brick wall. In situations like this it's very good to be able to let go.

Don't fight yourself needlessly, it's a waste of energy and will do more harm than good. Sometimes, because of a deep-rooted block, a goal that we set and don't seem to be able to reach should be persevered with. We have to be directed by our inner guidance. After a while you get a strong sense of what is positive for you and what is negative. We begin to realize when we are barking up the wrong tree. It's so hard to be honest and see through our mind's natural talent for living in a world of fantasies. It's surprising how many people do know on a deep level when they are in a situation that needs changing, or when they are pursuing the wrong goal. That's why self-awareness is so important, as we watch ourselves and learn about who we are, we know more and more about how to be and what is right. Negative patterns are outgrown and fall by the wayside.

When we set goals that are a natural expression of us and the way we fit into the world, we must be successful for we are resonating with life. We are in harmony, we grow. So when you decide what to visualize and affirm for, try to allow your life to unfold in a gentle and healthy way. Don't force things, yet at the same time, take risks and open up to the new. You are trying to create; we are creating the whole time anyway, but now you can see how your thoughts and feelings dictate so much of your life. Look at nature, see how a tree grows, imagine seeing its whole life cycle in a couple of minutes, all the seasons of new growth and death followed by more new growth. That is the pulse of life. Allow that pulse in you to express itself in the way that it wants.

The best and most productive way to set goals varies from individual to individual. Use your intuition, open your eyes and look at your life. It's an adventure, and an adventure always involves a lot of unexpected experiences. Find your own way, to discover and learn for yourself. Good luck.

Blocks and how to clear them

Sometimes when we are doing visualizations and affirmations to achieve a certain goal, it seems as though we are getting nowhere, even when we feel very good about what we are trying to do. It may be that we are going against the flow and it is pointless for us to carry on. However, often this is not the case, it's just that we are 'blocked'. We have negative patterns that actively prevent our success. There is an easy technique that allows us to locate our blocks and begin to release them, for seeing them is the first step to letting go and changing the way we relate to them.

Obtain two pieces of paper and a pen. Relax. Write on the first piece of paper the goal which you are trying to achieve. Now think about all the reasons you can't reach it. Be honest with yourself. Most of us at one time or another are riddled with negative self-doubt, for instance in a relationship situation, our observations may be simple like, 'I'm scared to open up' or 'I get too jealous', or we may see quite deep patterns such as, 'Because my last boyfriend was so cruel, I now feel hurt and unable to trust men, even though I realize that I created that feeling of hurt as much as him.'

General blocks are often along the lines of, 'Life isn't meant to be that good' or 'I'm not lucky enough' or even 'I don't deserve it.'

Whatever the situation, write down all the negative patterns you can dredge up regarding attaining your goal. Take some time.

When you have finished putting your negativity on paper read it through. All these attitudes are unnecessary. Look at them, feel how useless they are. You can be totally free of them. Rip up the piece of paper and throw it away, and as you do feel those negative chains smashing.

Now on the other piece of paper write down all your positive patterns and feelings. For instance, harping back to relationships, we might put, 'I have a lot to give' or 'I'm a sensitive person and love sharing this' or 'Because my last girlfriend and I had such a good sex life, I now feel confident sexually.'

Write down your goal and all the reasons you can think of as to why you will achieve it. Take some time to finish. You can also add to great effect positive affirmations such as:

'I am totally open to this goal.'
'Positivity guides me to attaining my desire.'
'The past is gone and I am totally open to the new.'

You can repeat this block-removing exercise a couple of times but that should be more than adequate for any particular goal.

Awareness of the past is, in itself, a change of the way the past affects you, but the best way to move on from negative patterns is by changing the way you relate in the present — to sort out negativity, focus on positivity.

How often

There is a lot of misunderstanding about how regularly it is best to undertake visualizations and affirmations. It is true to say that the mind is a creature of habit and due to this the regular repetition of any working will have a strong conditioning effect.

One person I know used to get up in the morning and spend one hour visualizing and affirming. They would have affirmations written by the bed, on the fridge and anywhere else they looked at often. During the day they would mentally repeat affirmations many thousands of times. Back home at night they would spend hours carrying on the good work — or so they thought. Whilst these massive doses of programming may have had a strong positive effect, they are also quite likely to go against you. One of the reasons is that when we are visualizing or affirming we are trying to gain access to the deeper areas of our mind. If we continue to be conscious of what we are trying to do in a specific working, it can prevent our intent or will from taking effect.

Be sensible. Obsession is not healthy, for the greatest chance of success it's good to cultivate an attitude of wanting and believing, yet at the same time not being too 'attached' to the result. If you are emotionally concerned about whether or not you will achieve your goal, any negative worries will block your chances. One hour to one and a half hours a day is more than enough to devote in total to your efforts. Obviously if you suddenly have 10 minutes on your hands, it can be an ideal time to do some affirmations. However, it should be said (although many may disagree) 30 minutes a day is plenty for someone who properly understands the underlying principles of visualization.

The best way to look at it is as follows. With specific workings, i.e. trying to get a new job or relationship, etc., it is definitely a help to 'let go' of your visualization once completed. Let it pass into the magic regions of your mind, but repeat everyday, once or at the most, twice. Remember to forget about it in between.

We are not saying that you shouldn't have a positive awareness all the time, just that visualizations and affirmations are generally more effective in 'short sharp shocks' regularly repeated.

As stated a few times previously, we are all different, and you could find that five hours a day is the optimum period for you to visualize and affirm, while for others five minutes once a week might work wonders. Try these things out, see what suits you best. Find out what is natural.

In sorting out our particular goal we should be guided by the individual dictates of each situation. 'Necessity is the mother of invention.' Sometimes a specific goal is appropriate, sometimes not. If in doubt, use a symbolic goal as well.

Attitude

Our attitude when we do visualizations and affirmations is incredibly important in determining the effects of our endeavours. Think of it in terms of vibrations. The visualizations and affirmations form a vibration, a pulse; the stronger, clearer and more charged this pulse is, the greater the chance it will create. Because of this our thoughts and emotions at the time of doing a working have a powerful effect.

We must want what we are trying to achieve. Implicit in this wanting is our acceptance of receiving it. If we are not truly open to receiving something, we don't really want it. However, often part of us wants it and another part doesn't. Because of this it can be very helpful to look at our acceptance as a separate concept. We may be blocking ourselves from positivity.

Belief is also very important; we have to believe that what we are trying to create is possible. Remember, the more positive we are the greater our chances of success. The greater our belief, the more charged our pulse/vibration is. So try and emotionally charge that vibration. Feel, desire, want, accept that what you want will happen, have no doubt, assume totally that you will be successful.

These concepts come together as will or intent. Our will is our centre of consciousness, the spark that is the life force in us. Techniques help us to focus it. It is our life direction, our creativity. Desire and believe what you will.

Acceptance

Acceptance, as a separate concept, is very significant. Some people think that will or intent is composed of three elements: desire, belief and acceptance. As previously mentioned, if we truly desire or want something enough, it is implicit that we are open to accepting or receiving it. For instance if a friend of yours offers you a fiver, if you want it you will take it. However, often our feelings are not that resolved. For instance, we may feel as though we want a good relationship, that is our conscious intent, but on more deep subconscious levels we might have all sorts of attitudes and patterns that prevent us from achieving a positive relationship. In these cases we are in a state of conflict: part of us wants X, part of us blocks X from happening. It is often quite rare that we are in total union with ourselves. In instances when there is conflict it is often productive to work on our acceptance consciousness with affirmations like:

'I am totally open to accepting a good relationship.'
'I accept a good relationship.'

Dividing will into belief, desire and acceptance, or just into desire and belief, makes little or no odds, they are just different ways to cut the same cake. Structures that explain things are just structures. Think of all the different psychological theories that describe the human mind. They are like mirrors that reflect what they are describing. Different mirrors reflect the same thing in an individual way. One is not necessarily 'better' or more 'accurate' than another, for the reflection is never the reflected, it is an image of the reflected. Do not try to hold onto an individual mirror, i.e. conceptual structure; see it for what it is, and learn through its angle of truth.

Spirituality and visualization

The quality of our vibration is all important. It is necessary to examine how pure your intentions are. Why do you want these things that you do? When you do a visualization, try to feel open to creating realities that are positive and healthy for you. Open your heart and have that genuine openness. It's so hard to know who and what we are and what is right to do. Openness is so relevant to change or growth.

There are no easy answers. So many books these days claim to explain the unexplainable, to put the mysteries of life into convenient words and phrases. What about visualization, where does this fit in? It has an immediate attraction because it offers us the possibility of directing our lives by our will. In a sense it offers us a chance to get in touch with our own 'godness'. Properly understood, techniques can give us tremendous power to create changes in our lives. That's why morality is needed to use visualization wisely. The author does not mean the generally accepted concept of morality with the division of right or wrong. It is not as simple as that, there are no hard and fast rules. It is our individual responsibility to find out and learn. Most people think learning has an end, but quite the reverse is true, learning is continuous, it goes on and on ceaselessly unfolding. The present always exists — through creating with the present we can learn about what actually is.

Visualization is a curious thing. If we are aware and sensitive, we do not need to visualize or affirm; no such mental tomfoolery is necessary. The people most able to visualize and affirm with any degree of power are, paradoxically, the least in need of doing it.

When we open our minds and learn, life unfolds naturally. However, for the vast majority of us, this is not the case; we are, to a greater or lesser extent, riddled with conflict and confusion. Practical visualizations can give us some stepping stones out of our own personal mire, but they are not the 'answer'. There can never, ever, be an answer.

Meditation and higher wills

We all know that we have some sort of personal will. For most of us this is composed of quite selfish impulses. Many people think that there is a spiritual or higher consciousness within us. This higher power has a will or intent which is somehow more altruistic. It is obvious to see these beliefs in people who are religious, i.e. 'the will of God' or some god-like or spiritual force. What is definitely true is that we are pretty unintegrated generally, having all sorts of conflicting desires and instincts. If we take the time to reflect and meditate, it's often very surprising how we can tune into our inner selves and find answers to problems in the sense that we get in touch with deeper feelings that are more meaningful.

Because of this, many visualizers find it extremely beneficial to 'ask their higher selves' for guidance. That's why it is common amongst different spiritual paths to find meditation as a requirement. It is almost impossible to develop psychologically and spiritually without some sort of meditation. On a simple level, spending half an hour every day to reflect and tune in allows us to clear out our minds and keep ourselves new. This freshness is imperative. How do you feel when you wake up? Do you feel alert, sensitive and eager to live? Or is the clutter of yesterday pressing down on your head with all those little fears and worries? Creativity is always in the present and is always new. Anything that helps us be in the present and relate in a fresh way is helpful to us.

In the next chapter a couple of meditational techniques are given. However, we must realize that meditation in its truest form is not confined to half an hour in the morning or evening, it's totally ongoing, an awareness that sees, responds and lives fully with what is.

Abundance and nature

The world has the potential for everyone to be living with all their needs met, since it is so abundant. Nature is plentiful and supplies us with much more than we need. It's so easy to forget how important nature and the elements are. Everything in the world, no matter how 'man-made', is created using natural elements. Man is rather like the magician in the Tarot; this card shows a magician standing behind a table on which are the four elements. He is free to combine them in any way he chooses. His will leads to his choices.

Look at how we have combined the elements of nature — cars that cost £100,000, for instance, all that energy and manipulation to provide a vehicle which we value in monetary terms when millions are starving. This is not an attempt to be judgemental here; it is necessary to remember, however, how the world has, in terms of its resources, more than enough for all of us to live abundantly. However, the way we use these resources is not all that positive. If you are doubting this so-called abundance, go into the country and look around you; nature constantly grows and renews itself — it is the life force itself. Tiny blades of grass can push their way through lumps of concrete.

Modern prosperity consciousness is full of writers going on and on about how the universe is abundant and we are all entitled to an enormous piece of this pie. This, to a certain extent, is true, in some way it is our birthright. But we should never forget the root of this. On earth it's very much connected with nature, and after all what is nature but life itself. It's all too easy to be clouded by what man has created, how man has used his will. To lead abundant lives, we need respect for the source of abundance.

Giving and love

When we give genuinely, it attracts a positive, providing energy into our life. A friend of mine, when he first came to London, would make a point of taking sandwiches and other foods to the homeless who slept under Charing Cross arches. He did so not because he thought it was a good thing to do but because he wanted to express a loving side of his nature. He gained as much from the experience as the people he was visiting. He had that energy naturally and because of this he was, to a large extent, looked after by life. He soon obtained a cheap flat to rent and a good job.

When people are cold and stingy, and we don't just mean materially, they create that energy in their life. If you want to be loved, love. Giving can teach us a lot and even if at first when we do it, we are not exactly sure of our motives, the process of giving can change us and alter us to experience new feelings. Look around you and see what opportunities there are to give. Some people give a proportion of their income, usually 10 per cent to an organization such as a charity or church. They feel much better for it, even if initially they started doing it for quite selfish reasons. Through doing it they learned to give unconditionally, which, when you stop to consider, is the only true way of giving. Can love have conditions attached? Do you expect something in return from the people that you love?

Unconditional love is a personal expression of true love. It's very hard not to be selfish, and a lot of us just learn to refine our selfishness in more and more subtle ways — but it's still there. If we are sensitive we care, we care from our hearts first. It's amazing how many people who are involved in politics or 'causes' take so little notice of what's going on right in front of them.

Once a friend told a story about how she was walking down the street and saw a van of political canvassers driving slowly. A guy was broadcasting messages about changing the world for the better and improving conditions in the Third World. The van stopped and everyone got out except this guy and his young son. The son tried to ask his father a question and the father immediately got angry and slapped him round the face. The boy started crying. This incident shows some important points. Here was this man apparently so concerned about the world, yet, right in front of him, he had no concern for his son. He could not see that he created the world, that the conflicts in the Third World were created by individuals like himself.

We create the world, so how we relate to friends and the people we meet, the vibrations we put out, are all terribly important. People under-estimate how much effect they have on life. They love to feel powerless to change anything, and they only concentrate on 'important issues' getting all steamed up, when they don't live in a positive, loving and creative way in their immediate surroundings. Change is immediate movement. By being more loving we can change the world right in front of our eyes. How we perceive, to a certain extent, creates what we perceive.

True love is never demanding, it does not ask to be accepted. It just is, like a flower, its being is its gift — it's up to us to look and see.

CHAPTER FIVE

PRACTICAL VISUALIZATIONS

This chapter contains visualizations and affirmations for all the various areas of our lives. Some of them just require you to relax and use your mind. Others use very basic paraphernalia that give a ritualistic effect. There are also some written passages on the different parts of our lives, so that we can understand the context of ourselves and what we are trying to achieve more clearly. Don't forget that if you are unsure or worried about the possible effect of a working, use a universal affirmation (page 47). *How* you relax is up to you. As previously stated, it's quite feasible to undertake most visualizations whilst sitting quietly in a chair. Other methods for deeper relaxation are given in Chapter 2.

How to start

At first it's often good to select one area that you feel most needs sorting out, but this is entirely up to you. Try to choose times to visualize when you know that you won't be disturbed — some people even take the phone off the hook and if possible switch off the doorbell. Mental attitude is important. If at the back of our minds we can't relax because we sense someone might come round or ring up, this can prevent our total attention on our visualizations. Anyway, enough words. The best way to start — is to start!

Relationships

Relationships of a sexual and deep emotional nature are what will be discussed. As with other parts of our life, we carry around many unnecessary negative patterns that hinder us in our ability to have positive relationships. Look around you — how many good relationships do you see? A relationship is only as good as the individuals in it. Remember the jigsaw analogy at the beginning of this book. Couples are rather like two pieces of a puzzle that fit together. In this alchemy some of the 'locks' are negative patterns. For example, there might be a bloke who has been conditioned to treat women badly. He expects to be able to get away with a lot and finds intimacy scary; so whenever things get too close he shuts off and detaches. He will attract that situation into his life because that is who he is. He may well magnetize himself towards a woman who has a complementary negative pattern, i.e. someone who expects a man to treat her badly and cut off when she gets emotional. These two people would fit together but not in a healthy way. People tend to take the role of least resistance and do not like change. Obviously in most relationships there is a mixture of positive and negative alchemy. What is important to finding out who we truly are is to examine our behaviour patterns. That's why awareness is so good, for we can watch ourselves and discover.

A large part of the way we relate to our partners is conditioned by our primary relationships with our mothers and fathers. What we learn at an early stage is often what we create later on. Although awareness of the past can help us to free ourselves from it, it is in the arena of the present that all change exists. We must be prepared to take that leap into the unknown to grow. Relationships can be very beautiful, exciting and constructive, but to find a relationship like this we have to 'create' these energies within ourselves. What we want, we must be.

Finding a partner

If you are alone and want a relationship, try this visualization.

Relax. Clear your mind and think about your desire for a relationship. Really feel it, build up the emotional charge. Now visualize the partner you would like. If there is someone in particular that you already know of then visualize them. Otherwise just visualize the sort of person you would like to be involved with. Along with the mental visual image of what the person looks like physically think of all the qualities you like in that person. Do not worry if it's hard to get a clear mental image. List all the positive attributes in your mind, muse them over and, most importantly, feel them in your heart.

When you feel that you've covered enough positive attributes of your prospective partner, think of all the things you enjoy or would enjoy about a relationship. Two or three will be enough to start with. Imagine doing those things with a partner. Once again strength of emotion is very imperative to charging your vision. Really feel as though you are with that person.

So to summarize, you create an image of the person you want, and then a vision of the two of you together having the relationship that you want. Add affirmations if you wish. Remember, when you visualize, feel it as though it were happening now, not in the future, but NOW. Feel it as though it does exist. Believe that it does. You can use this method to enhance an existing relationship as well.

Resolving a relationship

So often in a relationship the two individuals are stuck in a state of some sort of conflict that is unsatisfactory. Neither person seems able to move on and they both hold each other in limbo. The situation could be anything — someone keeps having affairs maybe, or they keep having the same arguments about the same petty issues. Nothing will change unless something in the relationship moves on. This 'something' usually is one or both of the people involved. Conflicts are never resolved at the same level at which they arise.

This visualization was created to resolve relationships. Implicit in this resolution must be the openness to the relationship ending if this is the most positive way for the two of you to go. It's good to have the desire and belief that it will work out, but sometimes the only creative solution is to grow apart.

Relax. Clear your mind. Feel love for your partner. Concentrate on all the loving feelings that you have, although you may have other negative feelings put these aside for the time being. Let your feelings of love and warmth flow through your body. When you feel bathed in positive love visualize your partner. See their face and see their eyes. Try to remember what their eyes look like. Use a photo if available to help you. Look into their eyes and feel love. Sense love from them. When you feel calm and peaceful say internally to yourself and whilst looking into your visualization of your partner's eyes:

'I am totally open to our relationship being resolved in the most positive way for both of us.'
Then imagine your partner replying, 'So am I.'

Repeat this a couple of times. Try to feel that openness from your heart, feel that unconditional love that means that although you want it to carry on, more than this you want the most positive resolution for the two of you.

Secret forces of nature

This is a powerful visualization to enable us to find a partner or lover. It can also be used to help an existing relationship.

To do this you really need to be sleeping alone. Before you go to bed close the bedroom window. Once lying down relax and think about the sort of partner you wish to meet. It cannot be stressed too strongly that your emotions are of primary importance in this. *Feel*, dwell on your feelings for a few minutes, totally assume and believe that life can provide you with what you want and need. If you are already in a relationship and need it to be sorted out in some way, visualize how you would like it to be.

Now, with both situations, when you have finished get up slowly and stand by the window, imagine at the moment your desires and beliefs are contained in you, when you open that window you will make a special connection with the outside world, the world that is going to provide you with what you want. Take a deep breath and open the window slowly, sense the outside air coming into your bedroom. Breathe slowly and visualize and feel your desires and beliefs mingling with the subtle currents of the world. Feel in your heart that you have made that connection.

This visualization is often most effective when undertaken sporadically. Once a week is enough. However you can increase its effect by looking forward to that time. Be excited by it, make that practical visualization into a powerful ritual that has a lot of meaning to you. When you breathe out and mingle your energy with the outside air, feel open in your heart to receiving what is the most positive for you. Every time you complete this visualization sleep with the window open if at all possible. Even if it's just a slither open have it like that, as while you sleep your subconscious will sense your openness to getting what you desire.

Invoking gods and goddesses

To attract yourself into a relationship, what you need to do is to find a god or goddess who in some way symbolizes the sort of partner you want to magnetize. For instance, if you wanted a boyfriend you might choose Apollo, or if you wanted a girlfriend it might be Aphrodite. Use any mythological system that you feel comfortable with. Myths have an amazing effect on our deep minds, as the stories they tell are stuffed full of archetypes which still have a strong relevance to human nature today. In our subconscious minds are all sorts of shared archetypes, a sort of collective subconscious. So once we have chosen our mythological partner, relax. Visualize if you can an image of the god or goddess you have selected. Use photos or drawings to help you if you wish. As you visualize say internally:

'I invoke Apollo [or whoever you have chosen] into my life.'

Really feel as though you are invoking, for you are. Carry on visualizing for a couple of minutes and invoke again. Repeat once more.

Properly done, this practical visualization will not take long to take effect. You will vibrate that archetype within you and consequently in the external world. Twice a week is enough, but do invoke three times when you do do it. If you don't have much luck with the particular god or goddess that you choose, try another one. Read about the myths that are associated with whoever you choose.

Heart technique

This is a visualization that can be used to help attract a relationship if you don't have one, or if you are already involved with someone, it can improve and enhance it.

Obtain a piece of red paper or card, some scissors and a pen or pencil. Relax, cut out a heart from the paper or card.

To attract a new partner
On one side of the heart write out your full name. Then write out all the good qualities you have to offer in a relationship. On the other side, if there is a particular person you wish to att-

ract write their name; if there isn't, don't write any name at all. Next put down all the qualities you desire from a partner. Try to put down things that you have a strong emotional desire for.

When finished add some positive affirmations on both sides, for instance, 'I magically create a positive relationship' or 'I attract with a burning desire my perfect partner.' When your visualization heart is completed you can keep it and 'charge it up' by taking it out every day or every other day and reading through and feeling what you have written.

To enhance an existing relationship
Here the method is pretty similar except obviously on the reverse side from yours write down the specific name of your partner. As before put in all the positive qualities you both have. When you come to add the affirmations, use ones that will help your relationship develop and grow. For instance, 'Every day this relationship constantly grows more positive' or 'Our love for each other is abundant.' Keep the heart as long as it *truly* works positively for you.

Affirmations for relationships

'I have a totally satisfying relationship.'
'I have a totally satisfying relationship with ... .'
'(Your name) and (partner's name) experience a wonderful relationship.'
'We love each other deeply.'
'Every day my relationship constantly gets better.'
'My love for ... develops beautifully.'
'I am open to receiving a good relationship.'
'I receive a lovely relationship.'
'I attract with a burning desire my perfect partner.'
'My relationship evolves wonderfully.'
'I am open to love from ... .'
'Love from ... pours into my life.'
'I magically create a positive relationship.'
'I desire and accept ...'s love.'

'I receive unlimited love from ... .'
'I give unlimited beautiful love to ... .'
'My heart is full and I radiate love to ... .'
'Pure, divine love guides this relationship.'
'I accept life from ... .'
'I give life to ... .'
'The universe constantly meets my emotional needs.'
'The universe constantly meets my relationship needs.'
'I magically attract ... for the good and love of all.'
'I attract a brilliant relationship.'
'I passionately love ... .'
'I am full of unconditional love for ... .'
'The universe protects and nurtures my relationship.'
'I embrace with all my being this relationship.'
'Infinite positive love creates a special partner for me.'
'I attract a full-on sexual and emotional partner.'
'I am open to a lusty, exciting relationship.'
'I meet my perfect partner.'

Sex

Sex seems to be such a problem for so many people these days. Apart from the conventional morality about fidelity, even when two people are in a monogamous relationship, sex can be a real issue: why is this?

Sex is a form of communication, of sharing, it can be a very deep form of relating. Often intense feelings and emotions are channelled through sexuality and sex itself. In most relationships the individuals concerned do not realize that sex will often represent the communication in the other areas of their life. If communication is really bad it will usually block sex. In a sense, focusing on our sex life is often missing the point; our problems in this area often represent much more deep-rooted issues which have to be confronted first. People also get tangled up regarding sex because it is strongly connected to the pain and pleasure principle. We experience something pleasurable and we want to repeat it. This attachment to recreating something will often breed pain and conflict, since to a certain extent pain and pleasure are two sides of the same coin. Trying to recreate the past stops us from creating in the present and discovering the new.

Sex can also be transcendent in the same ways as a mystical experience or drug. It allows us to be free temporarily from the small 'me' or 'I'. We can lose ourselves, forget about our worries and burdens and be happy and expressive. Sex can give us a lot of life and be very creative. Because of this transcendent effect, we can start to use it in an escapist fashion, to avoid facing ourselves. Sex is mysterious, playful, joyous, emotional. It is base, earthy, sensual and instinctive — it feels good. We create what it is for us, it is life meeting life — an unknowable union.

Resolving sexual problems/enhancing our sexuality

Visualizations can be a useful tool for helping us in this area of our life. What we have to do is to have an image or idea of how and in what way we want to change. If we have blocks it is often good to try and find out how and why these came about. If the blocks are very deep-rooted we may need to seek some sort of specialist help. We must be open to moving on from conflict. Whatever is productive and helps us create moving on should be embraced.

Because of the very deep-rooted nature of some sexual blocks, it would be silly to expect them to dissolve during 15 minutes of visualization. *They may do* but if not, and you are still unhappy, seek help, be accepting of change and start to create change by initiating it.

Visualization for developing our sexuality

Relax. Visualize yourself having sex in the way you desire and that feels good to you. Really try to feel it and experience positive sexual feelings. You could imagine having sex with someone you know, someone you know of and find attractive, i.e. a film star or mythological figure, it's up to you.

Affirmations for sex

'I have a good sex life.'
'I feel good about my sexuality.'
'My sex life constantly improves.'
'My sexuality evolves freely and lovingly.'
'Pure love radiates throughout my sexuality.
'I magically attract healthy, positive sex.'
'I enjoy sex.'
'I love sex and feel totally open to express myself.'
'I love and accept my partner's sexuality.'
'I feel good about enjoying sex.'
'I communicate my sexual needs.'
'I have an exciting and lusty sexual relationship.'
'I attract steamy, passionate sex.'

Money

Money is a strange energy. We all have different ideas and attitudes towards it. Some of us think that we don't deserve it or that it is something that needs to be worked hard at to achieve. Try to have a look at your conditioning and programming concerning money. If you sincerely believe in your heart that you will never be rich and that the only way you can earn enough cash to live is by working exceptionally hard, then that is the reality you will set. However, if you believe that the world is abundant and that there is plenty of cash for you, and that this cash is easily obtainable, that is what you will magnetize in your life.

As an example of this, a friend told an interesting story. A modern metaphysician was sick and tired of listening to negative prosperity consciousness, so he set out to show that it is possible to receive a lot of money for doing virtually nothing.

He constructed positive affirmations to reach this goal: *he believed* that the world was going to provide him with ample supplies of money. Soon after doing this he was going out for a walk when he spotted a bag left unattended. Inside was several thousand pounds. He accepted it as a true gift from the universe. On a practical note he did wait for a few days and looked at newspapers and left a note by the empty bag before deciding to keep it, just to make sure. This little tale illustrates how belief and desire, as *will,* can work wonders.

Acceptance

To open up and acknowledge channels between you and the universe it's important to *recognize* when your visualizations and affirmations are working. One acquaintance would always pick up and cherish any money he found. Even when he was quite wealthy he would stop at nothing to pick up a one pence piece. When asked about this by friends he said that by collecting it he was acknowledging that the universe was providing. He was positively affirming by taking it that he was open to accepting what the world offered.

How to obtain money

Most people try to get money in the wrong way, they focus too much energy on it, and it is always a constant worry: 'I'm in debt,' 'I can't afford to.' In short they are a slave to it. They have a lot of bad feelings about the whole issue and, as a result, send out negative vibrations which carry on the whole miserable cycle. It is *possible* to achieve large financial success through concentrating solely on the object of being rich. But what kind of energy is that? If we focus instead on living a healthy, fulfilling, positive life then money will surely follow as a *by product* of us doing what we enjoy. Don't make financial abundance your *primary goal* unless you want your primary energy to be *financial abundance* — think about it, is that what you really want in your heart of hearts?

PRACTICAL VISUALIZATIONS

Keeping channels open

If you want money to pour into your life, pour some out. Create movement and happiness in your life concerning finance, be generous, eradicate negative attitudes. Expect money to come to you easily, and very importantly — enjoy it when it does.

Money and what it is

It's hard to see clearly about what money is. Many people feel guilty about having it, or even the thought of having it. They look at the poor people in the world and find it hard to reconcile what they see with their own wealth. Money, in a sense, is totally artificial, it has an endless supply. Having a personal fortune does not in itself mean that we are denying anyone else, we have to see what money represents, what it is.

Money is intrinsically worthless, it only has a value in relation to something else. What people want isn't essentially money — it's what can be obtained with it, what it can be *converted* into, what it can be exchanged for. Money is an artificial yardstick that enables us to make some sort of value judgement about what we think things are 'worth' in relation to each other. It's a form of comparison which facilitates the simplification of trading. It's the accepted language of buying and selling.

If we understand what can be converted into money, and what money can be converted into, we can see that our drives and instincts to make vast fortunes could directly help others. Try to see the insidious nature of how we relate to money. People who are poor do not really need *money*, they need the exchange value it carries. What's important is the *way* in which money is created in one's life.

Visualizations for money

This is to open up channels to abundant cash.

Relax. Imagine an empty treasure chest with the lid open. Now visualize a gold coin dropping in. It looks like treasure glinting on the floor of the chest. More and more coins start to fall in, suddenly the trickle turns into a stream and then a torrent. The chest fills up rapidly as piles of beautiful coins pour in. Feel how good it is to have all these golden coins. The chest is full to the very brim and still torrents of coins rain down. The pile spills over the edge.

This visualization helps us open our channels to receiving wealth. Add jewels to the coins if you wish. To enhance, add an affirmation along the lines of:

'I am totally open to receiving unlimited wealth.'

To extend this visualization, use your home in place of the chest. For instance you may live in a small flat. Firstly imagine coins filling up one room and then spreading right through your home. Feel excited and happy as these golden symbols pour into your life.

Money play

This little game was invented to free some of our concepts concerning what money is. You need at least two people and a note of a reasonable denomination, £10 for example.

One of you starts with the money, it is yours, you own that £10. Pass it to your friend. You have now given them a tenner. Actually feel that you have. They in turn should acknowledge that they have received £10 and are richer for it. Now they pass it back, feeling that they have given you £10. Take it. Keep doing this back and forth for some minutes. It is important to feel that you are giving and receiving. When you stop, work out how much money you gave away and were given. Suppose you passed it 50 times, that's £500 that passed through your hands from that one £10 note. Think how much money a note generates in the course of its lifetime. With more than two people you keep passing it around clockwise or anti-clockwise. The exercise also has a powerful subconscious effect in that it generates a vibration of money flowing rapidly.

Shopping spree

A simple visualization to help us receive money for all the things we need and want and more besides.

Relax. Think for a few minutes of all the lovely things you would purchase if only you had the funds available. Don't hold back in your imagination, as well as the immediate items you would buy if you had a bit more money, go many steps further, visualize that you do indeed have absolutely unlimited amounts of cash. You have an everlasting magical wallet that never ever runs out. It is always stuffed with big money notes. As soon as you pull a fistful out, more instantly take its place. Now armed with this shopper's miracle you go shopping as never before.

Start off with the small items you've been meaning to get for some time. It could be a new tin opener or a new pair of shoes — visualize yourself in the relevant shop gleefully handing over large bills at the till. You feel happy. Next move on up to those things you really want — a new car, tickets for an exotic holiday, anything that excites you and generates a lot of energy. When you've stocked up on these items, go for the full-blown ultra-luxury stuff — yachts, islands, houses: whatever you want, since you have enough money to buy absolutely anything.

Money box

This is a true practical visualization where our internal will is externalized through a solid symbol. We need to make or obtain a box which can be used for storing money. It could be anything from a traditional wooden or metal container with a slit in the lid, to any other sort of box that you feel is appropriate.

Once you have acquired your money-box all you do is save the money. Coins are good because they have a strong impact on our deeper mind. Thinking about how money came to be is revealing. Before money existed everything was bartered. People would swop so many sacks of flour for a sheep and so on. Precious metals were useful because they could be exchanged for a variety of things. There was a large demand and a limited supply and so money was originally created from gold and silver. Everyone wanted it, it was a much better and more convenient way to obtain what we wanted than carrying around sacks of flour. It became much more interchangeable than anything else because people were prepared to exchange their goods for it.

Whenever you feel like it, place some coins in your box. My brother used to have an old sewing box that he saved pound coins in. It used to look lovely with its complete layers of coins. Little by little it filled up. We worked out that when it was full it would contain £1,000. As you fill your box, feel good about it. Take pleasure in dropping money in. Maybe you know what you will spend the money on, maybe not. This is a very good practical visualization to do when you owe a lot of money as it helps attract money into your life. Most people in debt concentrate solely on paying off what they owe as opposed to creating wealth. It's always positive to save as you are building up and focusing in the right direction. To only concentrate on your debts is to only deal with the negative.

A good visualization to go with the money-box is to relax and sense the magnetism of the coins. See them as a magnetic force drawing more and more cash your way. You could even write out some affirmations and stick them in your box.

To obtain a certain amount of cash (1)

Firstly decide how much money you require, suppose £10,000. Then relax. Clear your mind and feel calm. Now visualize an envelope with a letter inside it. You open it and fold out the letter. On the top right-hand corner is your name and address, see it as clearly as you can. On perusing the contents you are amazed to see it is from the universe's bank manager; it reads:

> Dear ... (your name), the universe is delighted to meet your requirement of £10,000. It is already here for you right now. You deserve it. Yours ... (you can't make out the signature).

As you read it through you feel elated and surprised, try to really be totally open to it. Visualize a cheque made out to you from the universe for the amount that you want. To go one step further for each of these, you can actually write out a letter or a blank cheque. Make them as realistic as possible. When you have made them relax as deeply as possible and look at them, feel as though they are real, make them real. When you have done this you can enhance your practical visualization even more by posting the letter and the cheque to yourself. Be surprised when you receive them in the post. Repeat this a couple of times if it feels right.

To obtain a certain amount of cash (2)

Decide how much you want. Relax. Visualize a bank; it's no ordinary bank, but a bank where unlimited amounts of funds are available absolutely free of charge. Think of a name for the bank. See it in your mind's eye; it could be something like 'Universal State Bank' or 'Free Bank'. As you can imagine there's a bit of a queue inside but people are dealt with surprisingly quickly. Very soon you reach the cashier. He/she smiles and asks you how much you want. You tell them your requirements and immediately they get the right amount of money out. You feel great as they pass it over and off you go. As you walk out you feel lighter and grateful. 'It's all so easy,' you think to yourself. Now spend a few moments visualizing what you will do with the money.

To open up channels — tithing

To truly receive we must be able to give. Every day for a week at least give money to anyone who asks for it. It only has to be small amounts but don't turn anyone down. As you give it feel joyous and happy, see each occasion as another channel between you and the universe opening.

Money affirmations

'Stupendous quantities of cash flow into my life.'
'The universe constantly supplies my every financial need.'
'I am totally open to receiving unlimited wealth.'
'Money pours into my life.'
'I deserve abundant riches.'
'Money flows freely.'
'I am rich.'
'I have loads of cash.'
'I magically attract money.'
'There is plenty of money for all.'
'Money is abundant and I obtain it easily.'
'I love and enjoy receiving wealth.'
'Every day I prosper more and more.'
'There is an unlimited source of money.'
'I open up to the unlimited source of money.'
'It's so easy to be rich.'
'I receive endless amounts of money by doing what I enjoy.'
'I attract myself to money now.'
'I am incredibly wealthy.'
'I love receiving and giving money.'
'Day by day wealth comes my way.'
'I always have plenty of money.'
'I attract myself immediately to the most positive way of receiving huge amounts of money.'
'I am amazingly lucky and find money in beautiful and unexpected ways.'
'Suddenly cash falls onto my lap.'
'I am a powerful money magnet.'
'I enjoy earning £... a week.'
'I enjoy being rich.'

Remember, if in doubt about your true intentions, add the universal affirmation 'For the good and love of all' at the end of your affirmation sessions.

Health and healing

Health is an area of life that has received a lot of attention over the past few years. A plethora of different diets exist that are all supposed to be 'it'. Obviously what we eat can and often does have a profound effect on our health. However, it's amazing how important our state of mind is in determining our physical health. You will see keep fit fanatics who exercise for many hours a day and are totally watchful about what food they eat. Some of these people look absolutely miserable — even though to all intents and purposes they are doing all they can to be healthy, they still get ill. Why?

Our mind has such an importance regarding health, especially the attitudes we have. If we have a lot of negativity we attract that into our lives and one of the best ways to do this is through ill-health. We could say that positivity is life-expanding and growing in the way that it seems to be intrinsically. Negativity is anti-life. Because we are a form of life that is conscious of itself, we are able to create positivity or negativity. A tree will just grow naturally. We, on the other hand, are in many ways a lot more complex and this complexity makes it much harder to be natural, and to know what is good for us. A positive, happy state of mind is an asset in attuning to keep good health. For one thing, if we have a positive outlook we will naturally seek out healthy foods and do things that enhance our lives physically.

Exercise

Exercise is important. However positive our outlook is, regular physical exercise will increase our experience of life no end.

Unless you have experienced being fit you will not know what it feels like. If we are truly aware of our bodies, then we will naturally want to exercise. Try it for yourself and find out. Once you have tasted the sweetness of fitness you will always want it. Apart from the obvious physical benefits, you feel clearer mentally. If we are sensitive to life and care about being alive we will look after our bodies.

Diet

Diet is a different isue. Most people go astray in sticking to one diet. Certain diets have benefits which continue as you eat the required foods. However, the human body is an extremely sensitive biochemical organism, and its biochemical imbalances *change*. These changes are created by a huge variety of factors both external and internal.

The importance of this is that what may be the right foods one week, might be totally unsuitable the next. It is unlikely to be that drastic, but that example does illustrate an important point. Also, as individuals, although there may be shared dietary requirements, there will also be specific needs. As with most areas of life there are no easy answers, it's up to each person to explore what foods suit them best at any given time.

Healing

Now, more than ever, the world, and particularly science, seems to be a lot more receptive to the idea that people have some say in their own health. No doubt science will one day show explicit relationships between our states of mind and our physical health. This is an extremely complex issue and hard to see clearly. It would appear that our immune system is susceptible to our moods and general well-being. Being 'run down' can often lead to catching colds, etc. When people are depressed they do seem to get ill more often than when they are positive and happy.

The alternative health field has grown tremendously. Many

of these therapies like to 'explain' our illnesses in terms of our psychology and how we lead our lives. For instance, the classic one is cancer being caused by repression over a long period of time. Although there is truth in these explanations, sometimes they are a bit too convenient. Humans love to understand and make the unknown known. Because of this we feel better if we can put our illness down to something — it happened because of X or Y. There will always be a 'cause' but what that is is often hard to know. We have a tremendous ability to heal ourselves and others in many different ways: love and kindness are healing. We understand so little about the way our minds and bodies work, particularly on the level of subtle energies. Many cancer centres use visualizing techniques to help their patients to begin to fight cancer. There is no doubt that by having a 'strong positive attitude' we can often heal ourselves and others. Different exercises and techniques can help us have a 'strong positive attitude' and also help us channel it in a constructive way.

Visualizations can definitely have a profound effect on our health, especialy when we are ill, but if you want to really develop your well-being, exercise is invaluable. Once you have tried it you will wonder how you ever did without it. it makes you feel alive.

The science of medicine is about to undergo a tremendous revolution. The study of man on an electro-magnetic level has only just begun. Through this area the world of the mystic and the world of the scientist will finally unite. That is a truly exciting prospect.

Visualizations for health

Getting in touch with our bodies
This exercise helps to make a mental connection with our physical being. It can be done lying down or sitting.

Relax. Now feel your foot and your toes. Try to project your consciousness into your foot. This may seem a bit ridiculous at first. But it is totally possible. When we feel our foot we are in some way making a mental connection. Explore how much of your foot you can sense with your mind. Now slowly start to do the same with your legs. Feel them in your mind and expand that link. Gradually work your way up your body until your consciousness reaches its natural abode. As you do this visualization you may experience images of the inside of your body, you may actually get pictures of what it looks like inside.

If you find difficulties with this technique, start off by just doing one hand. Look at it then close your eyes and sense each finger and finally the thumb. You will find that regular practice will be well rewarded, and once you are able to go round your body you will be far more aware of it generally.

White light
This is a visualization that can be used to heal when we are ill, and charge ourselves when we are healthy.

Relax. Whilst sitting down with your back straight, visualize a pool of white light at the base of your spine. Feel it brilliant and pure, sense it at the base of your spine. Take a deep breath and hold for a couple of seconds. As you breathe out, visualize the white light shooting up your spine and out of the top of your head, it cascades over your whole body. As you inhale, visualize the white light flowing out the base of your spine again. Then repeat as before, hold your breath for a couple of seconds and exhale slowly and strongly and feel that intense pure light shooting up your spine out of the top of your head and pouring over your body like a divine rain of brilliant droplets. Carry on for a few minutes with this white light bath. Just remember to 'see' the pool of light at the base of your spine as you breathe in, hold your breath and sense the energy. Then as you exhale, feel it streaming up your spine. If you like this exercise you may want to investigate some yoga techniques that involve deep breathing and muscle control with visualizing.

Healing ourselves and others

This is a powerful technique for creating and keeping good health. This method is the same for healing ourselves or someone that we know. Basically we create a positive image of whoever it is we wish to heal. Let's imagine we want to help a friend.

Relax. Visualize your friend looking radiantly healthy with a beaming face. It is often useful to have photos to do this. Try to obtain a picture that shows them happy. Concentrate with all your might on this positive image. Feel and see that they are well. If you are trying to heal yourself, use the same principle. Visualize yourself looking extremely well. As before use a photo to aid your image and add affirmations after your visualization to enhance the experience.

Going further from this, we can work specifically on the area of the body that is diseased. Relax as before, except this time visualize the diseased area and visualize it strong and healthy. For instance suppose we had a broken leg, we could imagine walking around on it and feeling good. When the illness is internal, such as a kidney infection, visualize the kidney looking well. It does not matter that you may not have a detailed knowledge of what a kidney looks like, it could be very simplistic; what is important is the feeling and energy that is behind the visualization. Add affirmations to enhance. Visualizing ourselves looking and feeling great is a good way to maintain good health. Imagine doing all the things that you really enjoy, see yourself happy in your strong, healthy body.

Athletic visualization

A visualization that helps us enjoy our bodies and extend our physical being.

Relax. Imagine that you are at the Olympics. What kind of sportsperson would you like to be? Suppose you've always fancied yourself as a bit of a runner, visualize yourself running in all the events you want. Hear the crowd, feel the excitement. You win a few heats and reach the finals. You feel nervous and look round at the other competitors. The atmosphere is tense and you're under starter's orders. Run as you have never run before, sense life bursting through your body as you finish the race. Did you win? You can use this visualization to act out all your sporting fantasies, you could even imagine receiving your gold medal and being interviewed on TV.

If the Olympics aren't your cup of tea, see yourself participating in any physical sport that you like. This technique is very useful if you do participate in a sport and you wish to develop and improve your performance.

Affirmations for health and healing

'I am radiantly healthy.'
'Life constantly replenishes my body and heals.'
'I am in perfect health.'
'I magically attract total health all the time.'
'The abundant healing power of love creates health.'
'I have good health.'
'My body looks, feels and is, exceptionally healthy.'
'My (whatever part of your body is diseased) attains perfect health and well-being.'
'(Name of person who is ill) magnetically attracts positive radiance and health.'
'I constantly eat the right foods to create health.'
'Pure white light pours into my body and heals all.'
'My inner power heals abundantly.'
'Unlimited health and strength streams into my body.'
'I deserve absolute well-being.'
'I have a strong healing ability.'
'I create the power to heal (name of person who is ill).'
'I am naturally healthy.'
'I totally heal (name of person who is ill).'
'I love my body.'
'I attract vibrant health.'

'I feel so strong.'

'Everyday, positive health flourishes my way.'

'Intuitively I attract and create total health.'

'The healing energy of life always keeps me well.'

'The healing energy of life always keeps (name of diseased person) well.'

'I only know absolute health.'

'Moment by moment, my radiant health and well-being grows.'

'(Name of diseased person) is very well.'

'(Name of diseased person) creates radiant health.'

'Divine healing energy vibrates throughout my total being.'

How to stop smoking

It is beyond the scope of this book to examine serious drink and drug addictions, but smoking is worth looking at separately because compared to other drugs, it is not nearly so mood altering.

It is very helpful, when we wish to stop, to understand that most of the time when we feel like smoking, we are just trying to relieve the symptoms of nicotine withdrawal. This lack of nicotine when our body is accustomed to having it makes us crave a cigarette. The important point is that we are not craving nicotine for the positive or pleasant effects it has. We desire it to *relieve* the sensations of not having it. Once this is truly grasped we can see how the whole cycle was set up when we first started to smoke. Do you remember how foul those initial cigarettes tasted and felt? After a couple of days the physical symptoms of not having nicotine disappear. We are then left to deal with the psychological addiction in which part of our identity is smoking. We link it subconsciously and consciously to certain thoughts, feelings and actions. For instance, we light up with a drink or when we are on the phone; because of these associations when we stop we may feel like smoking, because that is what we *know*. Although we feel like doing something, it does not mean that we have to do it. We can relate to those feelings in a new way. We can create a different way of being. The new will always push out the old. That is the natural movement of life. Smoking is anti-life, inside you know that it is bad for you and that you want to stop. Allow that impulse to catch fire. Change always means stepping into the unknown. When we change and totally want to do something, there is no choice. For we feel as one inside. Therefore there is no internal conflict, just complete movement.

Career/work

People love to separate their lives into categories. Their career and relationships are the two most common. For some, work is just a means to earn money; for others it is an expressive and fulfilling part of life. Everything gets terribly tangled up by the fact that for most of us we have to earn a living, we have to obtain money. This need can often crowd and prevent us from doing the work that is most suited to us. Work as such is a funny concept. Really we should be encouraged from a small age to explore and discover what it is that we really love to do. Unfortunately this is not the case for the vast majority. How many people do you know who really love their jobs? We could say being alive is a life's work and part of how we express ourselves is channelled in a way that will enable us to earn a living. Most of us focus much too much on the material aims of working as opposed to the deeper needs to do and to be.

The structure of society and of most jobs is extremely dulling to the mind, repetition of boring tasks, hours that are far too long. There have been some positive changes and the incredible development of technology will mean, less and less, that we have to do menial tasks. But unless *we* change, nothing will. Look at a large multi-national company, it may employ thousands and thousands of people. Year after year different people leave, different people join. But the company as a whole has a conditioning momentum; its aim, its goal is to make as large a profit as possible, that is the primary notion or intent of most businesses. That's basic economics. Often when a company makes a change that is good for the environment, for instance, they are doing so because it makes sound financial sense.

For most of us, our career in its true sense is the closest we will get to finding our way in the world, our reason for being. This is the positive aspect of what a career can be. Convention and the lack of good education at school does not facilitate us finding out what it is that we can have a passion for. Unless we get in touch with this, work will always be a chore. Have you ever noticed how, when you are getting paid for something you really love doing, it doesn't feel like work at all? If we concentrate on being ourselves, money will surely follow.

A friend of mine used to read Tarot cards. He saw thousands of people year after year. One of the most common questions he was asked was, 'Will I leave my job?' It's not up to the Tarot reader, it's up to the questioner. We love to avoid taking responsibility for our lives. We don't think we have a choice, we focus on *life happening to us* as though we have no say in the matter.

Creativity and joy are actively discouraged in most schools. Our education is, in fact, extremely narrow and academic. We are encouraged to develop, in a very specialized way, a certain part of who we are. We can break these terribly negative patterns, it is down to each one of us to search and realize what it is that we love doing. We must awaken and feel excitement and passion. Excitement creates. We spend usually half our waking hours doing work of some sort — that's a huge percentage. What we do, conditions us. It's no good expecting to be able to go to work and get it over with and then live the rest of your life. See your life as a totality, if you feel that sense of dread about going to work then something is wrong. Work is the most public expression of us, it is our worldly identity; he is a policeman, she is a painter. The difficulty lies in breaking away from the powerful values we have been conditioned with. There is so much admiration for status and money. To be free and happy we have to be prepared to be an individual, to stand out in the crowd.

If you feel stuck in your present work, realize that you will have to create something new. You can either relate to your job in a new way, or choose another. It's your life — it's your responsibility to live it to the full. That's what life wants to do, it wants to live and stretch, to expand and grow. Flow with that basic impulse. It's never too late to change. Often people only have the courage to move on when they are a bit older, because suddenly they see that if they don't soon, they will never have the chance. Intuitively we often have strong impulses and feelings about which direction we should go in — if you are lucky enough to have these, explore them, follow them through.

Another reason that people are scared of moving on is that they don't know what to do, and because of that they are insecure; they want to have something to go to before they let go of what they are doing. Obviously this is necessary occasionally because of practical considerations, but we may never have the time and space to find out unless we do let go. We must begin to explore the unknown. In the unknown all life begins. Do you remember when you were a child and the world seemed an incredibly exciting place? There was so much to do, so much to find out. The world is still like that, but you may have changed. It's the saddest thing to see the expression on some people's faces. They look dead and bland, pained yet numb. Life needs to change, for not to change is to die slowly from the inside. Most jobs are exceptionally static. If you are not happy with your working life *change* it. Be brave — be new.

Visualization for ambitions

This is an exercise that helps us to get in touch with what it is we really want to do.

Relax. Clear your mind and think back to when you were a child. Recall what it was that you thought you would do when you 'grew up'. Most children have many different ideas. Start off by trying to remember the earliest directions that you had when young. Gradually move up the years, feel and internally explore the various ambitions that you have had, and finally look at the present — what do you want to do now? As well as exploring your work/career/life ambitions, think back to what you really enjoyed doing when younger.

Hobbies

Hobbies are often an excellent way for people to express something they feel vital about. Although some turn to hobbies to kill boredom and don't really enjoy them, many find an incredible amount of satisfaction in having one. This is because they are doing something that they really want to. There is no worry about earning money because that is not one of the reasons that they are doing it. If you are bored at work, why not do an activity that you love? That energy will be very creative and can also be a practical way of exploring what you are into doing.

Many businesses start off as a hobby and gradually build up from there. Life seeks life, life creates more life — this cannot be stressed too much. If we have a positive expression, this in itself will rub off onto the other areas of our lives. We must stop splitting our lives up into convenient boxes. See your life as a continuous expression. Moment by moment we can hold life back, or let it grow.

Visualization to find a new job

This is a visualization to help us find a new job direction when we don't know what it is that we want to do. It will work whether we are currently working or whether we are unemployed.

Relax. Let your mind drift. You are walking down a country lane. It's quite narrow and lined with brambles and wild flowers, it is deserted and there are no houses about, just fields with some animals. The lane starts to descend towards an old well. You reach the well which does indeed look very old and notice a plaque which reads 'Work Wishing Well'. It goes on to explain that any wishes regarding work will immediately be granted. All you have to do is to speak into it what you desire. The well is your subconscious. Stand by the well and explain exactly what you want, if you are not sure just give the well as much information as you can. Make your wish. It could be something really simple like 'I desire a satisfying and fulfilling means of employment that is financially rewarding.' Speak your wish with total confidence. Once you have done this feel as though your wish has been granted. Feel totally open to receiving and accepting your wish happening in your life. Walk back up the lane to where you started.

Only do this visualization occasionally, at the most once a week. To enhance the power of it, add work affirmations that affirm what you had wished, for instance:

'I have a totally satisfying, fulfilling and financially rewarding job.'

To improve your work/career situation

Whatever your current situation, here is a visualization that can be used to develop it further in a positive way. Its power lies in the way it connects your mind with happy fulfilled energy in relation to your working life. You will begin to expect harmonious growth, and this expectancy will create it.

Relax and let your mind drift. Think about all the things that you really enjoy doing. This could be absolutely anything from painting, going to parties, eating, or even work itself. Spend a few minutes visualizing and experiencing those things in life that really excite you and give you a lot. Once you've thought of a few activities that you love, visualize yourself going to work, except this time you are being paid for doing all those lovely things you have just thought of. Visualize yourself in that situation, enjoying life and receiving a fat pay cheque at the end of the week or month. It's important to see yourself going into work in some way, and leaving at the end of the day; however short that day may be, it's up to you. Create an ideal working environment where you get paid as much as you want for doing what you love doing. Sense the joy in that. Add affirmations to enhance along the lines of:

'My work is totally satisfying and enjoyable.'
'I receive large amounts of money for doing what I love.'

To create a specific situation

This visualization can be used in a number of situations when we have a clear idea about what we want. For instance, we may be in a position and up for promotion. This visualization could help us attain it. Or we may be unemployed but we know the type of job we desire; once again, this technique will help.

You will need two pieces of paper and a pen or pencil. Relax, let your mind drift, muse over your current working situation. Think about all the things that you don't like about it and write them out. Take some time and try to be brutally honest. Really dredge up your negativity and earth it by putting it down in front of your eyes. When you have finished, read it through and throw the negative paper away after ripping it up. As you throw it away feel free of it.

Now, close your eyes and visualize as strongly as you can the situation that you want to occur. Feel what it would be like to be in that situation. Explore it as fully as you can. Charge it with the intensity of your desire. When you have done this for a few minutes, take the remaining piece of paper and write in large letters: 'I create this now.'

When you have done this, stare at what you have written, affirm it by saying it internally and out loud. Vibrate it. Feel the words vibrate through your whole body. You can repeat this exercise, but the next time only do the second half. For any particular situation you wish to create, it's only advisable to focus on your negativity once. Each time you have a fresh goal do the whole visualization, but when you want to carry on working towards the same goal just do the latter portion.

Visualization for career/work guidance

This is a visualization to help us get in touch with what it is we need to do to express ourselves in a fulfilling way through our career and work. More than this, it is designed to give us an overall view of our life, and what it is important to do in the larger context of our life direction, to hopefully enable us to find our vocation — our way in the world.

Relax. Imagine yourself at the foot of a large mountain. There is a long, steep, windy path that leads to the top. The sky is moody and overcast with sombre clouds. Start walking slowly and look at the flowers and bramble that flank the stony route. As you ascend you start to think about what you are doing with your life. At first the ascent seems a bit difficult, your footsteps are heavy and ponderous, however, after a little while you notice that your body feels lighter. The clouds begin to scatter, revealing patches of brilliant blue sky. The sun shines and sparkles as you carry on. You start to feel more and more positive. By the time you reach the top you are exceedingly calm and relaxed. The sky is an immaculate blue. At the summit you pause to catch your breath, you have a magnificent view of everything around you, you can see clearly. You sit at the top and relax. Ideas, feelings and prompting about your direction float up. You soon have a sense of what to do. When you feel like it walk down again.

Repeat this visualization every so often to attune yourself to your way.

Affirmations for work/career

'I have a great career.'
'I magically attract a positive career.'
'I am totally open to my way in the world.'
'I earn lots of money for doing what I like.'
'Every day my career develops with abundant positivity.'
'I enjoy my job tremendously.'
'I will my career to open up and grow.'
'I work at what I love and I love what I work at.'
'I attract the most positive career.'
'The universe guides me through my career and work.'
'I am totally open to changing my career in the most positive way.'
'Life constantly uplifts me through my work.'
'I express myself completely in my job.'
'I accept from the depths of my heart my way in the world.'
'Joy and abundance pour into my working life.'
'My career is incredibly creative.'
'I create an amazingly exciting and positive career.'
'I always know what I should do.'
'Love and divine light illuminate my path.'
'Life, show me my way now.'
'I am creating through my work.'
'My career brings infinite riches materially and spiritually.'
'My vocation constantly unfolds.'
'My career passion creates total positivity.'
'I do what excites and creates.'
'I evolve ceaselessly as life unfolds.'
'I magnetically vibrate my true vocation.'
'The universe constantly fulfils my career needs.'
'Happiness flows from my perfect career.'
'I earn pots of cash through my career.'
'My work is a pleasure.'

Love

Love means many different things to each of us. There can be many types of love — personal, universal, the love between two people in relationships, the love between parents and children, the love between friends. It is a complex emotion that varies from person to person. At its root is life having feeling for life. The type of love will often depend on the relationship between the two life forms. A lot of profound mystical experiences are due to people understanding and experiencing the source of life within ourselves.

On a more recognizable level nearly everyone wants love in their life, whether of an intimate kind or just more positive and loving relationships with the people we come into daily contact with. Every moment is an opportunity to create more love. As we give so we receive. If we go around full of anger and hostility we will vibrate these into the world and create anger and hostility. If we have love, we create more.

As we mentioned before, most people are quite demanding when they 'love'. They expect something in return. True love is unconditional, its joy is in its being, it does not need an answer, its fulfilment is its expression. Often when people meditate or have other experiences which put them in touch with the deeper levels of their being, they have contact with a source of what is experienced as some sort of love. Some describe it as the life force, universal or divine love. The essence of life itself. These deep feelings can often heal us and guide us in our lives. True love is always unknown, it is the essence of life which is constantly evolving. We can only touch it by letting go of experiences and by being the experience itself.

Sometimes people feel as though they are channels for this source. All sorts of religions and mythologies have complex words and theories to explain all this. What is important is not the various religions with their clumsy dogmas and rules, but what they are trying to explain. It is up to us to see the immense gap between the description and the described.

If we want to have more love in our lives then we have to start creating it. We could say that love is the most positive vibration. On a day to day basis there can be numerous opportunities to be positive, to enhance life generally. As soon as we get up we start to create, most people like to see their life in convenient segments, but it is a ceaselessly unfolding stream and as such, every moment is a creative opportunity. For instance a couple of cheery comments to the person in the newsagent's can start your day off on a good track. Have you ever noticed how, when you are feeling positive and happy, the world appears to be a positive and happy place? Love is as complex and mysterious as life itself, because in some way it is so closely linked. It can never be understood.

Visualization to create love in our lives

This is a powerful visualization that can be used to create whatever sort of love we desire.

Relax. Visualize a large white sunny room. There are beautiful windows, and sunbeams pour through. The floor is polished wood and the whole room is tastefully done with lovely simple furniture and harmonious textures. You wander around exploring for a couple of minutes. It's so peaceful and serene and you feel totally relaxed. It feels rather like a sanctuary in fact. There is a small table with some paper and an old pen. You sit by it and muse about what sort of love you would like to create in your life. Is it intimate relationship-orientated or just a general development of your most loving side? Sit in the sun and feel love, create it. Write on the paper or the desk exactly what you desire, feel what you desire, as you write you notice the sun becoming warmer, the whole room fills with a beautiful warmth and heat. You finish writing and experience the passion of the sun which warms your heart. You feel totally open to everything you have started to create.

Affirmations for love

'I get all the love I want and need.'
'I am a divine expression of love.'
'I attract love into my life.'
'I love and receive love.'
'Moment by moment love pours into my life.'
'I am totally open to the infinite love in the world.'
'Incredible amounts of love stream through my consciousness.'
'Unconditional love is all I seek.'
'Life is full of love.'
'I vibrate the highest love.'
'I am a channel for the divine love of the universe.'
'The evolutionary pulse expresses itself through me.'
'Every day I create and receive more love.'
'I am radiant, filled with light and love.'

Happiness

Happiness is a feeling. A lot of people try to 'be' happy, or they try to 'obtain' happiness. We could say that happiness is a state of mind, but for most it is a by product of what they are doing with their lives. A new job may 'make' someone happy, or a good relationship. Because of the elusive and somewhat nebulous nature of happiness, it is not nearly so easy to set goals, because what makes you happy varies tremendously from individual to individual. People conceptualize happiness in a wrong way, we all love to identify our feelings, but sometimes this labelling limits our experience of life. Often pleasure and happiness become confused and we get far too attached to what we think makes us happy. This attachment breeds fear of losing what gives us happiness. Happiness is categorized as a positive, desirable state, whereas sadness is seen as undesirable and something to be avoided. The truth is that our feelings, if we allow them, are infinitely more rich and subtle than words. In a sense, we cannot 'obtain' happiness, for you cannot hold on to it. Have you ever noticed how when life is going well and is enjoyable, we very rarely stop to exclaim 'I'm happy': we are too busy getting on with it. What a comparison to when we are depressed. Then all we can do is think of our ongoing misery.

Most of us find it hard to create happy situations in our lives because we are too attached to pain and confusion. This may sound unbelievable but please, look around you and see how people repeat the same negative patterns again and again. Why is this? To experience happiness we have to risk. To live, to open up to the new. Happiness will never be found in the past.

To increase happiness in our lives

You will need a piece of paper and a pen. Relax. Try to think of 10 extremely happy situations that you have had in your life. Or 10 situations you would really like to occur and which you feel would make you incredibly happy. It could be anything from going for a walk in the sun, eating a good meal, winning the pools, getting married. Whatever gives you happiness. Write them down on the paper. As you do sense them, imagine them happening now. Live them all and feel happy. After a while when you are feeling the sensations of happiness, throw the piece of paper away. Now, just sit feeling happy, vibrate it within yourself. Add affirmations if you wish.

Affirmations for happiness

'I am very happy.'
'Every day my happiness increases.'
'Happiness streams into my life.'
'I magnetize incredibly happy situations.'
'I attract and accept total happiness from the universe.'
'Happiness pours through my whole being.'

'My heart is filled with happiness.'
'I receive unlimited joy.'
'I create abundant joy and happiness.'
'I am happy.'
'Life is totally joyous and makes me happy.'
'Only happiness enters my life.'
'I passionately desire total joy.'
'My life is connected to the strong vibration of happiness.'

Spirituality

Spirituality in this context means trying to understand the source of existence within us. This is no simple matter. Visualizations and affirmations will make more sense and have more power if we see what they are. They are an internal vibration. Life consists of movement and the most basic way of describing movement is 'vibration'. Visualizations and affirmations are symbolic vibrations. They are to a certain extent dense vibrations. We give form to more refined and sensitive vibrations by internal pictures and words that we write and speak. It is necessary to see that these pictures and words are ways of creating with what we have learned and have been conditioned with. They are forms we have created.

We are all life that can experience life, a pinch of existence that is conscious of itself. Beyond these crude vibrations of pictures and words lies a world of subtle and infinite vibrations. Some people think that God is the source and that there is a sort of cosmic consciousness which is the most refined vibration of all. While this may or may not be true, we can say that we understand so little of what it is to be alive. When we express and channel the more subtle energies within us, we are attuning ourselves to the totality of life and how it wants to grow. Some would conceptualize this as the personal 'I' or 'will' identifying itself to the universal will. But this is a concept only.

Meditation

Meditation is a very useful way to explore the inner levels of our being. It is beyond the scope of this book to examine many methods of meditating. True meditation can be done at any time, a lot of meditational techniques actually dull the mind and repress it. They just give us another way of making existence known. Many of them work on the principle of distracting the mind so that the conditional known part of who we are is shut up by distraction, then hopefully we can experience the fullness of what we are beyond our own conceptions. Any image of life is the past, and a lot of people when meditating try to attain a certain state, a particular feeling or sensation, which they have experienced before. This defeats the whole purpose. True meditation is always fresh because when we truly meditate, we experience directly. The observer lets go of what he or she is observing and becomes it. Life unites with itself.

The limits of mental techniques

This impulse of life in humans to reach its source is so much more important than any visualization or affirmation. Awareness of creation within ourselves opens up the world. It gives us complete freedom. The mind thrives on habit and tricks which is why visualizations and affirmations work so well. We are able to reprogramme ourselves or, in a way, brainwash ourselves. But still we are approaching the problem from the outside, we are using a tool (the mind) which is, in itself, intrinsically sick. While not trying to devalue mental techniques, it is important to explore exactly what they are and their limitations. Our minds and the way we use them is the fundamental problem and although there is no doubt that visualizations and affirmations can bring profound and positive changes in our lives, isn't it purer to have a mind that is truly new and fresh, a mind that constantly becomes unknown. Can mental techniques do this? They may certainly help; but finally, even they are like a subtle shadow cast upon the truth.

Evolution — the movement of life

What is life and what does it want to do and be? If we look at the cycle of a tree, we can see the immensity of life, the 'pulse' that grows through birth and death. Life seems to move, to change, to expand, from the smallest cell to the universe itself which constantly stretches out. Life produces more life. That is its impulse, its will. This movement is evolution. Evolution is the direction of life. There seem to be some patterns which life evolves along, but evolution relies on the totally new. The new breaks with traditions and patterns, then there is true creation.

We are all a part of the oneness of life and surely our separate identity dies at death. Many people believe in some sort of reincarnation. They think that a part of us carries on, and it does, but not in the way that they think. When one leaf of a tree falls in autumn, the tree still lives but that individual leaf does not. Similarly when you or I die, our separation stops. The pinch of life that was conscious of itself ceases, but what it was conscious of carries on.

The life force is irrepressible, it dances through the seasons, it is constantly changing. What life is, who we are, constantly moves. Do we allow this movement to unfold and express itself in us? How hard it is to live, to express life, how easy it is to block it, to deaden and stop. True spiritual love is that profound connection with the movement of what is.

CHAPTER SIX

ADVANCED TECHNIQUES

By now we have more than covered the basics of creative visualization. This chapter has been designed to give you some really powerful techniques as well as guidance towards creating your own. We all have the potential to enjoy rich, fulfilling lives, however it's incredible how many of us cling to negative patterns of behaviour. Fear is often our biggest stumbling block; fear of change. Fear of what is, fear of moving away from our accustomed image of who we are. We love to identify ourselves, to say 'I am this' or 'I am that.' This is one of the most profound problems of life. We can be truly open to the new, vulnerable and trusting and living with a sensitive heart and mind, but because we are empty inside and don't really know ourselves we identify with whatever is convenient; work, partners or even possessions. That's why a lot of people are devastated when a relationship ends; they feel as though a part of them has gone. When we are more centred and in touch with our inner selves, we invest less and less psychologically outside of ourselves. As this happens there is an increasing openness to the world, due to fewer narrow and restricting beliefs about what life is and who we are. It will then be seen that we are a part of everything.

Life is constantly changing, bursting with movement. Look at the seasons with their beautiful cycles of death and rebirth. We are not content to flow like this and instead try to fix the flux, holding on and resisting change. Sometimes it's hard to accept things, and fear, when examined closely, is often a movement away from what is. In nature the new growth pushes out the old. In our lives, if we want to change, we need new creative impulses — visualization can plant these inspirational seeds. By getting in touch with higher sides of our being we can regenerate and live anew. We are only limited by our minds. Look around you and really see what man has done, see the world we have chosen to build, it's both wonderful and frightening. We all have a part to play, we are all creators. May your creative impulses be pure and divine, for the good and love of all!

TVV — television and video

This is a very powerful technique that can be used in a variety of ways. It was originally created to help people review situations in their life that they found painful and hard to accept. However, it can also be used to project into the future and positively visualize whatever it is you want to occur.

Relax. Close your eyes and breathe deeply. Imagine you are in the countryside. There is an old lane and you slowly walk down it, different flowers and brambles flank your side. The lane bends quite a lot, rather like a lazy river. After a while you spy a beautiful white cottage at the end of the path. No other house is in sight, and as you approach you sense that no one is inside.

You open the old wooden door and walk into an old room all white with the only furniture being an extremely comfortable chair that sits in front of a massive television with a video attached. The walls are lined with shelves and on them are thousands of video tapes. The whole room is chock-a-block. It looks like some sort of library. As you sit in the chair and glance round at the titles, suddenly you realize your whole life is in that room. Every experience you have ever had is there on tape. It's an incredible feeling as you look round. After musing a while you decide to leave. You get up and stroll out into the fresh air. The lane feels strong and earthy on your feet. Sense your feet on the path. Now feel them on your floor, slowly open your eyes. Breathe deeply.

Accepting the past

You can use this technique whenever you want to revise an event in your life. Maybe a situation where you didn't get a chance to express your feelings. For example, a relative died and you bottled everything up. Do the visualization as before but when you get into the video room pick out a tape from the shelves, see the title depicting whatever you want it to and imagine putting the tape in the video player. The television is huge and so the screen will virtually fill up your field of vision.

Watch that experience. In our example of a relative dying, you may see yourself at the funeral with all the family. Often powerful emotions will surface. Allow yourself to express whatever feelings you have. The tape will finish when it feels right to you. Looking at the screen releases you from that experience, and you can literally grow through things. So any situation or event in your life which you feel you haven't resolved can be watched again and let go of.

Enjoying memories

We can also use TVV in a much more playful way. Some people get out their photo albums to remind themselves of times gone by, well now you can go one step further! Any enjoyable experience you've had can be lived through again, in the comfort and privacy of your own internal cinema. Maybe if you had a relationship that was particularly inspiring and uplifting, take out a psychic video and watch some edited highlights.

Recording the future

TVV can also be an extremely strong tool for positively creating the future. Suppose you have an interview for a job coming up. Once in the video room, take out a blank tape, put it in. Now visualize on the TV screen how you would like the interview to go. The tape will record this. When you have finished, imagine rewinding the video. Now play it back and watch it. To really boost the effectiveness you can review the video a few times before actually going to the interview. In this fashion any future event can be 'recorded' before it actually occurs.

Psychic attack

It's amazing how often people think they are being attacked by others using some kind of magic! In my experience well over 90 per cent of the cases are no more than paranoia — someone who is feeling bad and wants to justify it in a fanciful way as opposed to facing themselves. What we think does affect others, and we have all been on the receiving end of a friend or acquaintance who is harbouring bad feelings towards us. They don't have to say anything — their expression is more than enough. People used to ask me to make them talismans for psychic protection. They sometimes had elaborate fantasies about others who were out to get them. There was often a lot of hate between the two parties, and this hate seemed to breed fear. I found a very simple technique which worked extremely well in nearly all cases of suspected or actual psychic attack. When we know someone who doesn't like us or who is directing a lot of anger and hostility our way, our resentment and own bad feelings only provide hooks for their aggression. If we can truly love and forgive them, all will be well.

Light a white candle, sit down and relax for a while, think of the person you have a problem with. Feel love for them in your heart — if you can't at first don't worry! Just say to yourself, 'I forgive (their name).' Look at the lovely softness and clarity of the flame as it moves. Feel the warmth and life. Five to ten minutes should be ample but continue for longer if you want. Repeat every day until you really feel forgiveness in your heart. When you start to experience that unconditional love, there will be nothing for their negative energy to latch on to. Forgiveness and love are the most powerful ways to truly protect yourself.

Power affirmations

We have already seen how affirmations can be a potent aid to creating the reality we desire. However they can be used in their own right, often bringing extremely fast results. First decide on your goal. In this instance let's imagine we need a new job. Now write out at least 15 times a positive affirmation such as, 'I have a job that is totally fulfilling spiritually and materially.' You can also try writing it in the second and third person, i.e. 'Chris now has a job,' and 'Chris, you now have a job,' etc. Repeat every couple of days if necessary. To really boost the power you can write them out with both hands; writing with the hand you don't normally use is extremely effective. Remember as before, it's best to write the affirmations in the present tense, this helps create results faster. You can also try different coloured pens for the various areas of your life. You choose the colours, for instance, you might have green for health matters. Whatever you think is appropriate — is.

Mantra affirmations

Mantras are very spiritual words or chants that are often used during meditations to attract, through their spoken or **silent** repetition, positive energy. They may be designed to solve a particular problem or they can be general, as is the case of a lot of religious mantras which are supposed to connect you to God, or some spiritual aspect of the universe.

The silent or spoken repetition of an affirmation is a vibrant way to obtain what you want and need. First of all, decide on the affirmation you wish to use. (Any affirmation will do.) Start off by saying it silently to yourself, keep repeating it and as you do, start to feel the vibrations of the affirmation until you can sense the sounds of rhythm of the different words. Focus more and more on the sounds and form and less on the actual meaning of the words. After a bit of practice you will quickly build up a distinctive mantra for any given affirmation. The finished product may end up as noises, with the words indistinguishable. Whatever you create is right. You can use this mantra whenever you have some spare time — going to work, after relaxing, during exercise. It will soon become second nature to go through it. You can also set the mantra to a simple tune. Once you have formed the mantra you can speak it, sing it, hum it or say it silently, whichever you feel most comfortable with.

Taped affirmations, normal and subliminal

Recently there have been an abundance of new tapes containing positive affirmations. Some are audible and some are recorded subliminally with a background of usually natural sounds. It's a funny thing, our subconscious, and it responds in different ways to different voices. However, without a doubt our own voice affects us in a very strong way. So, any affirmation you have you can record. For the best results use first, second and third person and speak in a clear, bright, positive voice. Remember that the vibration of your voice is strongly influenced by your mood, so do the recording when you feel joyous and positive. For any areas of your life that you wish to work on include some affirmations.

When the tape is finished you can listen to it at normal

volume whenever you feel like it. One hour a day is usually more than enough. But to really make them work play the tape at just below a reasonable audible level before/as you go to sleep. This way the sounds will travel directly into your subconscious.

Divination

Divination has been used since earliest times to look into the future. However if we analyze the word 'divination' we can see that it is related to the divine, and so in their highest aspect predictive systems can help us align our lives with the universe and our spiritual selves. The actual process of 'divination' can bring us good luck and inspiration.

Personal fortune cards

Here is a truly personal divination system that is great fun to use. Obtain a piece of white card large enough to cut out 10 Tarot-sized cards (approx 2 1/2in by 4in). Make them smaller if you prefer. These 10 cards are going to provide different answers to any questions you may wish to ask. Look at them as a private language, imagine the plethora of queries one can have: 'Should I continue this relationship?' 'How will I pay this debt?' 'What should I do in this situation?' So our cards will have to be pretty flexible to always be able to give a relevant answer. You could make two of them 'yes' or 'no' cards to give clear-cut answers, and also have 'death' and 'birth' cards as these will show beginnings and endings of things. It's useful to have 'happiness' and 'sadness' cards as these will show how things will affect you on an emotional level. You might want to have more than one meaning for each card. Write and/or draw the meanings on the cards. Use colours, symbols, words, whatever appeals to you. At first you might complete three or four cards, don't worry, keep these and add the others as you create them. Obviously you can have as many as you want; a Tarot deck has 78, each one different! To use your personal fortune deck think of a question, shuffle and select one or more cards, interpret them to answer your enquiry. Often one card is enough, particularly if it is very relevant to your situation, i.e. suppose you asked about leaving work and you got the 'yes' or the 'death' card. Or you were wondering about whether you should enter a new relationship and you got the 'birth' card. Although each card is autonomous you can create meanings for the combined influences of cards with each other. It's up to you! Be open and experiment to see what ideas work when you do a reading.

Receptive visualization

Relax and do some deep breathing, after a couple of minutes think about any question you would like to ask. It could be specific such as 'Will I pass my exams?' or it could be general: 'What will tomorrow be like?' Now close your eyes and continue to relax and deep breathe. In your mind's eye watch our for different images to come up. It may help to darken the room. After a while you will get images appearing, they might be very distant at first, they are often quite weird and disconnected. Try not to hold onto them but let them pass through your mind.

Any that seem relevant you can write down. For instance with the exam question you could see some papers with a pass grade, or you might see a large cross. However, you should remember that a lot of symbols and pictures that float up from your unconscious can be very irrelevant, rather like psychic garbage. The cross could just represent your fear of failure, likewise the pass grade could be your desire to pass. With regular attempts and by keeping a note of what you have seen and how accurately it turns out, you will learn to distinguish what is true prophecy. It is interesting to note that here we do not direct our visualization at all, we just watch it as it happens in our mind's eye. We can write out our questions beforehand on paper, as this helps us focus.

You can also use receptive visualization to get in touch with your inner feelings. For example, you could ask 'What will it be like if I take this job?' or 'How does he feel about me?' Relax and let your subconscious show you your deeper feelings in the form of pictures and sensations. Sensations are important as some people have difficulty in 'seeing' pictures — non-visual impressions are just as significant and informative.

Music and colour

Sight and sound are the two most powerful sensory vibrations. As such they have a strong effect on our lives, and by recognizing this we can use them to our advantage in visualization and affirmation.

Music

Music has a very emotive quality. It's quite interesting to note what kind of music different people like as it shows a lot about them — what sorts of vibrations they have. Music is very mood altering and so we can greatly boost and resonate workings by playing appropriate music while doing a visualization or affirmation. For instance, suppose we wanted to find a partner, we could play some atmospheric, romantic music. This would put us in the mood or set the right vibrations. Experiment and see for yourself how effective it can be. Also, as we become more aware, we notice the profound effect music can have on our consciousness. It's no good listening to loud discordant sounds if we are trying to be harmonious, it just won't work. So look at what sort of music you listen to and see what energy it has. Is it healthy? Does it create the feelings that you want? Remember, we are all a collection of vibrations, some of which are highly sensitive, so be aware of what you are vibrating within yourself.

One area music is undoubtedly useful for is healing. Some peaceful and beautiful music in itself has a healing quality. No doubt in the future medicine will make full use of the study of vibrations in relation to health. Use music for healing if it feels right for you.

Colour

Colour has a slightly more subtle effect, though sometimes it's quite obvious. As we go into a brightly-painted room we feel strongly, for example. The clothes that we wear can have a powerful vibration on how we feel. Have you noticed how some colours really seem to suit some people? They resonate and are in tune. Once we start to look at how colour affects us, it's incredible to see. Just because we were unaware before does not mean that colour vibrations had no effect on us, they just had a subconscious action. When people are depressed they will often choose to dress in black and drab garments. When people are happy the reverse is true. Colourful positive colours are cheerfully displayed. If we feel like expressing our inner selves through colour, albeit quite unconsciously, surely this shows that we have conscious and unconscious connections between the vibrations within us and the vibrations of colour. Experiment for yourself and try wearing different colours to see what result they have on your experience of life.

The world is composed of vibrations. We experience the world through our senses. Sight and sound are used the most often. By being aware of this we can learn about the interaction between ourselves and the world through sight and sound. As an interesting exercise, start to listen to the tone with which people speak. It's amazing to see the difference in energy. Feel the vibration as much as understanding the words. Being abroad is useful for this as with a foreign language that we don't understand, we can learn a lot from the tone and quality of the sound. The actual vibration of sound reveals a tremendous amount. Vibrations are the simplest form of movement.

'Yes' and 'no' divination with playing cards

Because of the sometimes nebulous results obtained through

general clairvoyance, it's extremely useful to have a divination system that gives a clear-cut 'yes' or 'no' answer. A pack of normal playing cards provides us with all we need. The basics are very simple: red is positive = yes, black is negative = no. Shuffle the pack thoroughly and cut. Depending on how important the question is, you will need to pick out different numbers of the same colour in sequence to get an answer. For example, suppose you were quite concerned about a particular question, you would keep turning over cards until you got three in a row of either black or red. If you got three red, the answer would be 'yes', if three black, the answer would be 'no'. If you didn't care that much about the question you might decide you only needed two or even one. Obviously you decide on the number before you start turning the cards. However if something really mattered you may want four or five cards in order. If you go right through the pack without getting the required sequence, shuffle, cut and try again. If after three times you have still drawn a blank, leave and enquire another time.

Fairy tales

Fairy tales can be very beautiful and often contain, in a simple form, powerful myths that reflect our lives. They can be used in a variety of ways with creative visualization. One of the strongest, and most lovely, is to write your own and in the plot weave in what you would like to happen in your life. Let's take the example of being single and wanting a relationship. Get a pen and paper, relax for a bit and then describe your ideal partner. If you want a male partner you could have them as a prince, likewise if you want a female they could be a princess. If you desire a particular person, you can make the character fit exactly. Otherwise with no one specific in mind you can describe them as you want. The images that come to mind often give clues as to what they will actually look like in real life when you meet. For a woman wanting a man the fairy tale might go something like this:

There was once a beautiful princess called (woman's name) who lived in an isolated castle with her rich parents. Although she had fine silk clothes and ample food her heart was empty. How she yearned for a dashing knight to ride into her life. Unfortunately, visitors were few and far between as her parents preferred their own company and seldom invited people round. One evening while everyone slept the princess awoke and looked out of her window, the moon was bright and kissed the trees with silver, owls hooted in the nearby woods and she felt a tingling of excitement. Suddenly the princess looked down and was startled to see a young man standing below in the garden. She didn't know what to do as he called up softly ...

This is just an example, write down anything you want. Use your own name and the names of other people that may be involved. For instance there might be someone you yearn after, so name the prince or princess after them.

You can also draw pictures to accompany if you wish. Artistic merit is not as important as strength of feeling. It may take a few days to finish this story, it doesn't matter! Let your imagination and creativity run riot. When you have a fairy tale that is completed to your satisfaction, write it out neatly and keep it. All you have to remember is to write a story which, in some ways, contains what you want to happen. What you want to happen could be absolutely anything. Create characters and objects that represent your life as you would like it to be. As you write it, visualize it.

Alternatively try this example. Suppose someone you know is ill and you want to heal them. You could pen a tale in which a magical doctor is found to assist. The doctor could be a wizard or any other image you have of a powerful healer. In your story he could administer a herbal potion that cured them very quickly. You could be the character that goes out and finds the doctor/healer. This example could work in two ways. Firstly, it may attract the right doctor into the real-life situation, and secondly, the actual process of visualizing the fairy tale will have a healing effect in itself. For best results it's a good idea to keep your fairy tales in a special place and to reread and visualize from time to time.

For those who find it a bit complicated to create a fairy tale it is suggested that you can write a descriptive story instead. It will work just as well. Another alternative is to imagine it's the News, and whatever you wish to occur is read out as a news item. In this case write it in a completely dry and factual way.

Health

We have already seen how visualization can be utilized to reach and maintain good health. There are three techniques to help cure our disease.

Colours and shapes to remove pain

Here is a simple, yet quick, method for relieving pain. Firstly, sit or lie down and relax for a few minutes. Now sense and feel the pain; wherever it is in your body mentally make contact with it. What kind of colour (or mixture of colours) does it seem like? In your mind's eye a colour will appear. Once it has, see what kind of shape it is (it could be irregular or regular). Mentally translate the pain into a colour and shape, feel the pain being represented by that image. If you can't see a colour, select one at random and choose a shape for it. The energy of the pain will start to translate itself into the colour shape. The pain will start to go. With a bit of practice this can work wonders and will usually be effective the first time you try it. You can also visualize the colour shape going out of your head and floating away. As it does, feel the pain travelling with it.

Intuitive healing

Different techniques allow our natural healing energies to come through and be channelled in a focused way. Many healers do seem to sense a sort of universal force, or love, that flows. That energy is very pure and strong. Although techniques can help us get in touch with that energy, it is the healing energy itself that creates healing, not the method used to structure it.

The most powerful way to heal is to express that energy directly. This expression will vary from person to person. One way is to feel love; it's as simple as that, as love and compassion are essentially healing. If you truly understand this it doesn't matter if you are actually physically with the sick person or not. (A photo is a good way of making connection.) Feel the universal energy which is beyond personal love, direct it to the person who is ill. This cannot be described in a way that is easy to follow, you have to intuit it. Allow that sublime force to float through you. Feel your way into it. Some people 'see' the energy as a certain colour, others just 'know' it's there. Let your intuition guide you as to how you should express it.

Food and health

Our attitude when eating really does affect how much energy or prana we obtain from a meal. Even if we have to consume something we normally wouldn't touch, a calm respectful manner will help ensure that maximum benefit is derived.

A simple ritual to translate the positive energy from food to any given part of our body is as follows. When you are ill, before you eat relax and do some deep breathing. As you eat feel the energy and power of your food, feel it in your stomach, imagine the energy being released into your body. (Some people find it helpful to visualize the food energy as a white light that flows down their throat and spreads out in their stomach.) Sense the healing power coursing through your veins. Now direct it to the part of your system that is diseased. For example, if you had a broken ankle you could visualize it flowing down your leg and circulating in a brilliant white pool around the break. Feel its soothing and healing qualities. If you have a general illness that affects your whole system you could imagine the white energy circulating right around your body. When ill, you can use this ritual every time you eat.

Talismans

Talismans are a magical way of making a symbolic representation of something you desire. They are a bit like subconscious telephone codes, the code being a set of symbols which connect you with what you want/need. The stronger the symbol, the more chance it has of working. Traditionally they are drawn on parchment, but nowadays paper is normally used. In their most simple form all you would have to do is to draw and write what you wanted on a two inch square of paper. The size of the paper can vary — whatever is convenient.

Let's take, as an example, a situation in which we needed to find somewhere else to live. We can start off by drawing a symbolic house on our chosen piece of paper. What other symbols might we use? A key? A removal van? We put onto the paper anything that suggests or symbolizes moving home to us. We would also write down our desire as well. Probably we'd sketch the type of place we wanted, and/or the area we may wish to move to. Take your time, it might require a couple of sessions to finish it to your satisfaction. When it is done, you can charge it up by holding it in your right hand and visualizing your goal. You could then carry it round with you or keep it in a safe place, fold it if necessary. Every day you can charge it as before. You could also add positive affirmations about your aims. For relationships we could make the talisman heart-shaped. A money talisman could be drawn onto a bank note. Be imaginative. If you are concerned about the possible outcome of any working, write down the universal affirmation — for the good and love of all. This will ensure a harmonious result for you and everyone else involved.

Intuitive vibing

The techniques we have looked at so far have all clothed our will or intent in various symbols and words. However, the purer vibrations within us are beyond conscious definition, that's why we have to give them some sort of crude form such as a picture or a sentence. There is an extremely powerful way to create changes and that is to intuitively vibrate the energy that we wish to bring into our lives. It is a sort of meditation which explains how meditation can have such a profound effect. When we meditate we are relating to ourselves and life in a different way. We let go and allow deeper energies within us to come out and express themselves.

Suppose we set our goal, it could be anything. Relax. Now feel your way into the situation or vibration you want to create. Pictures and thoughts may well float up as you attune yourself, watch these images but try not to hold onto them. Let them pass. Try to intuitively find the vibration that feels right to attain your goal. Sometimes you can sense that you've clicked in to the right energy. There really is no other way to describe it. Once you have found it, vibrate it and resonate it. Here we are going straight to the purest vibration, our will/intent creates directly, with no interference from cloudy subconscious images.

Ritualizing our actions (1)

Visualizations in themselves are usually very powerful. However, there are many ways to enhance their strength. Atmosphere and mood have a strong effect on our state of mind. For instance a romantic dinner for two is a very strong ritual, and as such has a lot of ingredients that help create a certain ambience. Soft lights, maybe some music, good food, we have probably taken an effort with our dress and appearance. All these factors have a subtle influence on our behaviour. So we can ritualize our visualizations and increase their energy.

Here are some suggestions for ways in which you may like to consciously use rituals: by lighting candles, having a bath or shower before starting visualizations, having special clothes to wear for psychic work, having a special room, or if that's not possible, a part of a room, using music to create atmosphere, burning incense, wearing aromatic oils, doing your visualizations at a particular time, following lunar cycles; in fact anything that you feel helps you focus and create a magical mood. It is useful to be relaxed, yet attentive, with a heightened state of awareness. Our minds quickly become accustomed to habits and so if you have a schedule or ritual before doing a visualization, the starting of that schedule will automatically start to create the right mental attitude. For example, if we always light a white candle before a session, after a couple of weeks the lighting of that candle will in itself trigger off a calm yet concentrated atmosphere in our minds.

Ritualizing our actions (2)

When we are engaged in some activity that isn't too demanding mentally, we can connect affirmations and visualizations onto our actions and use that energy. For instance, once I was clearing away some branches in a friend's garden. It involved bagging up a huge pile of dead wood. At that period I was going through a lot of changes, and although the major decisions had been taken there was a lot of leftover stuff to deal with. It struck me that removing the dead wood from the garden symbolized how I needed to clear up the dead wood in my life. So as I started to put the branches into the bags I felt myself trying to clear things up. I created a positive affirmation to help me be open to change and achieving my own goal of tidying.

Any every day action can be used in this way — cleaning, washing, running, walking — just mentally connect what it means or symbolizes to you. A couple of examples should help to illustrate this. Suppose you are trying to get promotion at work, and you had come up against a couple of obstacles. One day while walking to work you decided that this journey from home to work would represent your journey to promotion. Thus the route symbolizes your desires and barriers. You may well find that as you consciously do this some event happens on the way and gives you an understanding of how to resolve your obstructions.

Alternatively imagine you've just finished a relationship and wanted to let go of your ex-partner. You could wash all the clothes you wore when you were with them. The washing would symbolize you being cleansed of the negative effects of that relationship. Many people use rituals like this a lot of the time without realizing it. One person I knew used to go to the toilet whenever she wanted to let go of something. As she peed she would visualize the negative energy going out of her body and then she would flush it away. Awareness of our actions gives us endless creative opportunities.

Omens

Omens can provide us with astonishing insights into how our visualizations have gone. They can also show us how situations will develop in our lives. Omens can be defined as an event or occurrence that has particular symbolic significance. For instance, we may have just finished a visualization to obtain money, we feel good about it and go for a walk; just outside our home there is a £1 coin lying shining on the pavement. It catches the light and glistens as we pick it up. It is obviously unusual to find a new coin, but particularly so when we have just been doing a financial visualization. The new £1 coin sitting in the sun is an omen, a sort of symbolic sign from the universe. We would obviously feel very positive and may interpret the omen as our visualization is going to work — indeed it already has.

Alternatively use this example: you go on a first date, the meal is great, the atmosphere good, on leaving the restaurant a flower vendor comes up to you both and gives you a flower saying, 'Ah, the perfect couple.' This would obviously be a very auspicious omen. So, after you have done a visualization look out for some sort of symbolic event that might give you a clue as to how things will go, or what you might have to work on to reach your goal.

If you are interested in finding out more, there are books with lists of omens and what they mean. For example, an owl is often considered wise but unlucky, a four-leaf clover lucky. What is important is how the omen feels to you at the time. The context and your experience matter, not what somebody else thinks. Often we attract omens to guide us. We might have an interview for a job we are not sure about. On our way we suddenly realize that we have forgotten to put on the right shoes, there isn't time to go back and we feel terrible — maybe subconsciously we know the job isn't right for us. Don't look for omens too often. It's far better to have a few clear-cut signs than to try and interpret every little happening in our lives.

Finally

We have reached the end of our little guide to the creative world of visualization. The ideas contained in this chapter have been selected to help you realize your own. Don't be afraid to explore and experiment — there are no rules as to what you can and cannot do, that's your responsibility. The world is an incredibly mysterious place, and we could all be so alive and sensitive. The only limitations are our minds. Techniques are just tools for leading and inspiring us to creating directly with life. We should never become too attached to the tools we use.

When we dare to truly open, we meet the intense passionate flame of evolution itself.

The truth of what is, has a beauty beyond words.
May you find it now.

MODERN SPELLS

These spells have been designed for life today. A spell is a bit like a subconscious telephone code, the code being a set of symbols which connect you with what you want/need.

A spell is a vibration and as such can have a strong catalysing action on our life. Spells are a natural extension of practical visualizations. It is hoped that they will show the link between traditional occult techniques and modern visualization as they both work along the same principles.

Sometimes the symbolism of a spell is made clear, at others it is left behind. This is deliberate. When we are told, for instance, to repeat an action seven times, the unconscious and conscious mind may 'project' a meaning and importance onto the number seven whether or not any was intended, thus giving a powerful ritualistic significance.

Hopefully by trying some of these spells you will be encouraged to make some up yourselves. It's fun, and personal symbolism is very creative.

I would like to take this opportunity to thank Timothy Turner, a friend of mine, who collaborated on much of the material in this section. I wish him all the best in his new life.

Once again if you are worried about the possible outcome

of any spell, use the universal affirmation 'for the good and love of all'.

A

Ability: To increase ability in general, find a quiet place where you will be undisturbed and look into a mirror. Mime the task that you will have ahead of you in front of the mirror. Repeat seven times.

Affair: To create an affair, make a cup of tea or coffee with one more teaspoon of sugar than you normally have. Change the colour of the sugar as well, i.e. if you usually take white have brown and vice versa. (If you don't have sugar, have one of either variety.) Whilst drinking this, gaze out of the window, gently swilling the cup round in a clockwise direction. Keep a cup prepared in a similar way beside your bed at night. Have one cup, window gazing, once a day. Results should hopefully be obtained within two weeks. The sugar represents variety and spice and the window ritual symbolizes you being open to new people in your life.

Alternatives: To increase alternatives in your life, for two days each week vary your normal routine as much as possible. Get dressed in a different way, have a different breakfast, go to work on a different route or buy a new mode of transport. Talk to different people, have an unusual lunch. Do something in the evening that you wouldn't normally do. Have one item for dinner that you have never had before.

Awareness: Read a book on religion/philosophy or psychology every two weeks or two months. Then read any book by J. Krishnamurti.

B

Back: To bring back something or someone that has gone from your life, tie an elastic band around a coin tightly. Cast this coin into a stretch of water. The currents of water will undo the band from the coin and the universe will decide if and when your loss is to be released from its present state of bondage.

Bankruptcy: To get out of bankruptcy, light a white candle, take a low denomination banknote and burn it, and throw the ashes away. These represent the bankrupt state that you find yourself in at the moment. Now find a large empty jar and drop some coins inside. Every day add some more coins. When you have gathered sufficient coins, start to use these (sparingly) to purchase small items connected with your efforts to sort out your finances, i.e. pens, paper, envelopes, stamps and fares for journeys. These special coins should speed things up and attract further income.

Boredom: To break away from boredom, try staying in bed all day. You should only leave your bed to eat, wash, etc. Odd as it may sound, this is actually a strong 'reverse' spell. By opting to take this feeling to its extreme you will quickly realize that boredom is a mask for something else and that you have the power to change it.

C

Cake: To bring together two or more elements in your life and integrate them thoroughly, for example a work situation and a love situation, take the ingredients of your favourite cake and write out a list of the ingredients in two columns, each column representing one of the areas you wish to integrate. If you wanted to blend three things together you would divide the list into three. Once the cake is baked, eat it over a period of days. This symbolizes you taking in and digesting and integrating the various elements in your life.

Comfort: To comfort and heal yourself, go to a park on a nice day, sit down and relax in a place which feels special to you. Sit for 20-60 minutes (longer if you feel like it). When you leave, take something natural from the place, a leaf or a blade of grass for example. This symbolizes you taking the healing energy of the park with you. Go back as much as you want. Each time return the last item you took and pick up something new when you leave.

Communicate: To receive communication from another, go out to a phone box and feed it with enough coins for a local call. The coins should be given to you freely from another person (you may ask for them). Dial the speaking clock and note the time accurately, including the seconds. Write this down and seal it in an envelope including the date. Place this under your pillow and the magic will begin to work.

D

Debt: To get out of debt, obtain a building brick. Place it under your bed. This brick symbolizes material security and the element earth. Each night just before you go to bed, take it out and run the second finger of your right hand lightly along each of the six faces of the brick. Replace the brick and go to sleep.

Deceit: One way to try and make someone tell the truth is to buy a small, cheap hand mirror and take it to the person in question. Show it to them and ask what they think of the quality, ask if they think it to be a good reflection. Once they have looked into it ask them the question that you wish to know the answer to.

Decipher: To decipher a happening in your life or to resolve a conflict, go back to the time of the event and work out the initial source. For instance, if someone has walked out of your life go back to the exact time that you first met them. Try to discover what brought you there. If you can, repeat the journey/mission and see what is there. This can give you a key to the future.

Dream: To dream of a particular person or place, repeat the name concerned internally to yourself at least 1,000 times one day. Use this spell sparingly.

E

End: To end any situation, go to the very end of a particular route, i.e. bus or train, go the last stop on the line and make sure that you haven't been to this stop before. Get out and say out loud, 'I want this situation to end now.' Go home and allow things to be resolved.

Engagement: To fulfil an emotional engagement between two people, obtain some plasticine and roughly shape out the hand of your desired partner. Then do the same with your own. Place a symbolic eternity ring on each third finger of the hands, and entwine the two hands together by the fingers. Place in a large biscuit tin or similar container and fill with household salt. Wait and see what happens. Remember to dismantle the spell after the event.

Envy: To decrease this feeling in yourself, try this simple spell. Seek out from your possessions a treasured item such as a book or record. Give this to someone you are envious of and try to give it with good spirits.

F

Fate: To change your fate, one Saturday (the day associated with the planet Saturn) take a coin and, using the code tails for left and heads for right, go out of your house and flip the coin. If it's heads turn right, if tails turn left. When you come across a possible turning you can choose to flip the coin or you can go straight on, it's up to you. This spell symbolizes you being open to new influences and directions in your life.

Fate: For another spell to change your fate, wait until there is a visible new moon in the night sky and then find the seven brightest stars that you can.

Feel: To enhance and get in touch with your feelings, stay up all night and watch the sunrise. Go to bed later on in the day.

G

Ghosts: To get rid of unwanted ghosts, light a white candle in the room nearest to the ghost or spirit. Before you do, however, you should tidy up and clean the room thoroughly, then sprinkle a small amount of salt in each corner and splash some pure water on each surface of the room. Feel the gentle strength of the candle and let it burn right down. Say a prayer and ask the ghost to leave.

Gift: Use this spell to pass a message or feeling to someone. Of course, it's much better to tell the person face to face but if you can't bring yourself to do this or if it's inappropriate you can give them a gift which symbolizes what you feel. A common example is flowers, which usually symbolize love. You have to work at your own personal code. Giving someone a pen, for example, may indicate that you want them to be more precise and sharp in what they want from you or how they relate to you. If they accept your gift it signifies that they are prepared to accept your message or what you are offering them.

Guidance: To receive guidance when you feel lost, visit somewhere you have never been before and wander around until you are lost. It is important that you do really get lost and do not know where to go. (Obviously it would be silly to go somewhere dangerous.) When you are lost, say to yourself aloud, 'I am lost.' Then ask for help until you find your way back home. Wherever you go, make sure there are lots of people there. On your way home, look out for a sign or omen that could give you guidance in your situation.

H

Habits: Use this spell to break habits. The best time to break habits and to start on a new direction is the day of the new moon. Any new moon will do. This is the beginning of a new cycle and will help you a lot if you try to start something on this day or the couple of days following.

Halloween: To see your future partner, just before midnight on Halloween sit in front of a large mirror. The only light source should be a candle in a traditional carved-out pumpkin or swede. Look with your eyes half-shut in the mirror. It is said that if you are going to enjoy a strong relationship during the next year you will see an image of your partner in the mirror.

Hallucinate: Everything we see around us could be described as a positive hallucination. To be able to see a simple object such as a cup we need to have enough information about the object to form a belief. If you think about this you can see how powerful the forces of belief and imagination are.

Headache: To get rid of a headache get a glass of hot water and drink it in small sips. This usually works (although sometimes two cups are required).

I

Images: To see images, paint a normal plate with two coats of thick, black matt paint — the stuff used for blackboards is ideal. Sit in a darkened room and relax. Take some deep breaths. Now take the plate and place it on your lap or on a table in front of you. Gaze lightly into the middle. After some time and practice images should start to appear. It must be stressed that for a lot of people much practice may be needed. This method of clairvoyance is an alternative to using a crystal ball. At first only use for up to half an hour at a time. In occult circles this is known as 'scrying'.

Immediate: To act immediately, obtain a box of matches and think of what you want to do. Light one match and just after it has flared up blow it out. Repeat this 18 times, making 19 strikes in total.

Isolation: To get out of an isolated state, get five smallish branches (about one foot long and not too thick) and on the first day snap one in half. Each day for the next four days snap one more branch in half. The branches represent your internal isolation. Then after five days burn all the pieces of the branch. Then to make the magic really work, you must talk about your feelings of isolation to five different people. By the fifth person your feelings of isolation will have changed for the better.

J

Jewellery: Jewellery is often used in 'psychometry' readings, as the vibration of the wearer's life has been absorbed by the jewellery. To enhance good vibrations, gently stroke a ring or other item with love, using the right hand. To feel the vibrations of a piece of jewellery, place the item on a flat surface in front of you. A table is best. Then hold your left hand over the item with the hollow of your palm over it. The left hand is traditionally the receptive hand, so with practice you will be able to sense feelings. You can also hold it in your left hand to receive impressions.

Jobs: To obtain a job if you are unemployed, go out of the house at 9 o'clock and come back at 5 o'clock every day for a week. By doing this you will be 'plugging' into the subconscious wave of society of the people who are working. While you are out of the house, job hunt. This spell should work within two weeks and should ideally be started on a new moon.

Joy: To increase joy, buy or obtain six different kinds of flowers and place these in six vases. Keep the vases in the main room of where you live. Wait until the petals start to fall. Keep one petal from each of the six different flowers. These six petals should then be dried and sewn up inside a little cotton bag. The bag should then be hung up inside the main room of your home. Add a few drops of perfume to the sachet if you so desire.

K

Karma: This is to help change your karma although it should be pointed out that karma is instant — what we do creates who we are instantly. However, this may obviously affect our future. Walk backwards for at least a quarter of a mile. Be careful. With each step you take, think about how you felt in the past and how you would like to make changes now and for the future.

Key: To increase general fortune, have three copies of your front-door key made. Open your door three times with each one and then bury the keys in a large triangle around your house. Make the triangle as large as possible as this could be interpreted as your area of luck influence. You can even go to other countries to bury them as long as your house is geographically roughly in the middle of three buried keys.

Knowledge: For two hours a week wear a blindfold and think about the topics you would like to know more about. Relax your mind. Wearing ear-plugs may help.

L

Ladder: To master superstitions, deliberately walk under the next three ladders you pass. After this walk under or around ladders, depending on which is more convenient.

Law: To sort out legal problems, obtain a low denomination banknote, get a quill and use lemon juice instead of ink. On the note write details of your situation and put down that you wish it to be sorted out in the best interests of all concerned. Go to your nearest police station and donate the money to the police benevolent fund or some other police charity.

Leaf: To make a wish, catch a leaf as it falls from a tree. Wish as you catch it.

Love: To find true love, wait until you are given a cup by someone. If this seems to be taking a long time then you may ask a friend to give you one. When you have received your cup go out and buy another one, the most beautiful cup you can find and afford. Do not bargain for it — pay the asking price. The cup is a symbol of love. Now get up at sunrise on a clear day and hold the cup to the sun. Imagine the cup filling with sunbeams from the morning sun. As soon as possible do the same thing with the moon at night. Hold the cup out towards the moon and imagine the cup being filled with moonbeams mixed with sunbeams. The sun is a symbol for the male and the moon is a symbol for the female. By blending them together in your loving cup you will draw closer to your true love. Repeat if required.

Luck: To increase your luck, try to carry out important activities on days which reduce to the same number as your birthday. For example if you were born on the second day of the month, use days 2, 11, 20. If you were born on the thirtieth, use days 3, 12, 21 and 30. If in doubt, consult a simple book on numerology.

M

Magistrate: To influence a magistrate (if your motives for doing so are honest), find out the magistrate's name and write it out backwards. Encircle it in ink of some sort (i.e. a pen). Then write out how you want the court case to go and what result is desired. Fold up the piece of paper and seal with wax. Place it in your right shoe when you go to court. Point your right foot at the magistrate and think about what you have written.

Marriage: To get married to a special person, buy some confetti and light a white candle. Say out loud the name of the person that you would like to marry. Then speak your wish. Get a wedding ring, now pass some confetti through the wedding ring. Blow out the candle. Every day (or as often as possible) go to the house of your lover and sprinkle a few bits of confetti around the entrance to their home. Every time they pass over the confetti they will subconsciously receive your message.

Music: To get in touch with someone urgently, pick out a song which that person really likes. Play it, and while you listen try to visualize their face whilst mentally calling their name.

N

Name: To try and divine the names of people who may be important in your life, on the first Wednesday of any month get up and go outside. The first name you hear mentioned will be important to you.

Name: For a long time names have been very revered in magic. If you do not like your name then it is suggested that you change it. It's quite easy to do. A lot of people would scoff at the idea that the vibrations of our name have an effect on our lives, however, it is possible to change your life by altering your name. It would be advisable to see a good numerologist if you seriously wanted to do this.

Negativity: To get rid of negativity, run a bath containing 10 tablespoons of salt. Stay in the bath for 15 minutes and think about any bad feelings that you want to get rid of. Try to pass them into the water. The next day, if required, have a bath with five tablespoons of salt.

O

Open: To open up any situation, for 20 hours do not close any doors. Open all the doors in your home (if safe to do so) and sleep with them open. Also open as many windows as possible.

Opportunity: To get a golden opportunity, obtain a small key, paint it with gold paint and wear it around your neck for a month — preferably starting on a new moon.

Oracle: To receive information about a particular event or time in the future, light a white candle and write down on a piece of paper details of what you want to find out about. Burn the paper but make sure you keep the ashes. Blow out the candle. Bury the ashes next to a tree, a tree that looks very healthy. Take one leaf or small branch from the tree. When you wish to dream about the event or time, put the leaf or branch under your pillow that night. Use for a maximum of three nights.

Oracle: To find out about an event or period of time, or to answer any question that you may have, obtain a magazine with lots of pictures in it. Light a candle (optional) and frame the question clearly in your mind. Then chose a number between one and the number of pages in the magazine, i.e. if there were 100 pages pick a number between 1 and 100. Just take the first number that comes to mind. Turn to that page, and the picture or information on that page should give you an answer to your question in either a literal or symbolic form.

P

Party: To clear a bad atmosphere in your home, throw a special party and only invite happy, positive people. This can clear out a bad atmosphere permanently. Perhaps this is connected with one of the reasons that people have 'house-warming' parties.

Past: To let go of the past, over a period of weeks write out a complete life history, recording all important feelings, thoughts and main events. Read it out to a close friend then throw it away. It is important to share it with someone else as this earths it and releases it.

Prediction: A simple way to make a prediction about a person is to search your memory for someone similar. Try and remember what types of situation they found themselves in and what happened. This is a useful basis for you to be able to pick up and understand patterns of behaviour.

Q

Quantity: To obtain a quantity or one particular item — for instance a book — go into a photo booth with one example of what you want. Take four identical pictures of yourself hiding the item in your right hand. Put the four photos in the corners of your bedroom.

Quest: To give you a new direction in life. Pick a day to go to the countryside. Take a bag with you. Collect seven interesting items. They could be anything, it's up to you to decide. When you get home examine them for signs or symbolic significance.

Question: To obtain a 'yes' or 'no' answer to a question, go into the road and note the first car registration number that you see. Add the numbers up. If the result is even the answer is 'no', if odd 'yes'. You can always work out quite a complex divinatory system using different specific numbers to give various answers.

Quilt: To change your life, buy a new quilt cover, bearing in mind that the pattern it has will symbolize the change that you require. For instance if you wish things to be more black and white and clear-cut, choose a cover with a simple black and white design. If you want more peace and harmony, choose a plain, pleasant design. If you want more love, choose one with flowers or hearts. Work out what you want to attract and select a design to suit. Because you sleep under it, the pattern you pick will have a strong subconscious effect.

R

Random: To live your life in a more random way or to introduce random elements into your life, obtain a normal six-sided die. For any decisions you have to make, write down six possible choices. Number these options one to six. Roll the die and carry out the choice it selects. If you only have two options, then write each out three times and number them in the same way. Use this procedure for when you have under six choices, just write some of them out more than once. For this die ritual to work, you must put down options that you are actually prepared to carry out. Try to be adventurous and use common sense.

Reality: To see reality, do not do any of the following for one day or more: watch TV, listen to the radio, listen to any sort of music, go to any films or any form of entertainment. Do not read anything, do not write anything. In fact do not have any distractions at all for one day. Do not do any work at all, if possible. Watch your thoughts and see what you think about.

Religion: To break free from any cult or religion, pick the most important prayer or mantra, etc. from that religion, write it out backwards and speak it aloud three times, three days in a row. As you speak you can visualize large metal chains being broken as you are released from the dogma of that cult or religion.

S

Sea: To make a wish come true, write down your wish on a piece of paper, bind the paper to a largish stone with a rubber band. Throw the stone as far as you can into the sea. As the paper disintegrates and merges with the water your wish is released.

Sex: To overcome sexual difficulties, on a Tuesday write a letter to the problem page of a newspaper or magazine and outline your worries. Use a pseudonym if you want but give your correct address.

Stress: To reduce stress, write down a list of numbers from one to ten. Alongside each number write a word that you find relaxing. Memorize this list of numbers and words. Before you go to sleep at night just count from ten down to one and you should automatically start to relax.

T

Taboo: To release your inhibitions, write down on a piece of paper what taboos you would like to release. Bury the piece of paper at the bottom of a pot of rich earth. Leave the paper at the bottom of this pot for one week. After seven days dig it up and look at what's left, then throw it away. Tell one person about your taboo to complete the spell.

Telepathy: To increase telepathic powers, get a normal pack of playing cards. Go through them trying to guess what colour they are by looking at the backs. After practising this you can move on to guessing the suits and finally the numbers as well. It should be stressed that for most people a lot of time and effort may be required to get results, and due to this it may not be worth doing.

Trauma: To recover from trauma, go to the park or into the country. Find a secluded spot, take off your shoes and socks and sit down planting your feet firmly on the ground. Under a large tree can be a good place to sit. Breath slowly and relax, try to sense and feel the earthing power of the ground.

Travel: To travel well and without trouble, buy the smallest compass you can find. Before you go on your journey light a candle and ask the compass to guide and protect you on your travels. Somewhere on the compass inscribe by whatever means possible a number that is lucky for you. Blow out the candle. Take the compass with you.

U

Unconscious: To get in touch with your unconscious or subconscious, set an alarm clock for two hours after you have gone to bed. When you have woken set it two hours ahead. Carry on doing this until the morning so that by then you will have 'woken' three to five times during the night. This will help you to get in touch with your subconscious or unconscious. Repeat infrequently if required.

Uncover: To uncover a situation and find out information that will help you to resolve it, write down details on some paper and place on the floor in a secluded spot. Cover with cloth of some sort. Every day for the next eight days look at the cloth and think about the problem for a few minutes. On the ninth day take the cloth off and put the paper on a window. Over the next two or three days facts should come to light.

Undoing: To prevent a situation or set of circumstances from becoming undone, obtain a spare pair of shoes with laces and tie the laces up as if you were wearing the shoes. Keep the shoes under your bed until the situation is sorted out. Then untie them and put them back where they would normally be.

V

Victory: To attain a victory in a situation, take a largish piece of coloured cloth and make a flag. Stick onto a piece of wood.

On the cloth write down details of the situation in which you wish to be victorious. Then keep the flag-pole in a prominent place where you live, and pick it up in your right hand every morning and raise it to the ceiling.

Voices: To pick up spirit voices and/or interesting psychic phenomena, put a blank tape in a tape recorder attached to a radio or a radio-cassette. Tune the radio to a frequency that has a certain amount of static but no discernible radio station. Then leave the tape to record. It is best to do this last thing at night just before you go to sleep. Play back the next day to see what you have picked up. It might take quite a few times before you get any results.

W

Watch: To break free of the restrictions of time, buy a cheap wind-up watch with traditional hands and face. Wind it up and wear it. For three days look at the time a lot. At the end of the third day take the cover off and break away the hands. Wear and wind up for as long as you want. This symbolizes your desire to relate to time in a different way.

Will: To increase your will power, get a normal watch or clock with a second hand. Watch and concentrate on the tip of the second hand. Do not take your eyes off it. Watch it go round second by second. Start off by concentrating for a few minutes and after a while slowly build up to 30-60 minutes at a time. This exercise will improve your concentration and focus of will tremendously.

X

X-Certificate: To solve a dangerous or complicated life

situation that demands immediate action, get a magazine or paper that lists all the films in your locality. Close your eyes and run your finger down the listings. Stop at some point. The nearest X-rated film to your finger is the one that you should go and see. The film will show you in some way a 'message' to help you resolve your situation.

Xylophone: To enhance any spell, after performing it play a few notes on the xylophone. Try to make them as atmospheric as possible. As you play them sense the sound vibrating the spell into action. Improvise with vessels filled with water if a xylophone is not easily obtainable.

Y

Yes: To be more positive, on the mirror that you first see every day write the word 'yes'. On a piece of card the size of a playing card write 'yes' in large letters. Carry this with you and look at it 19 times a day for one week.

Youth: To understand about age and youth, talk to someone who is at least 20 years older than yourself for one hour a week. For another hour watch children play.

Z

Zest: To boost your zest for life, have as long a holiday as you can afford.

Zest: Again, to boost your zest for life, write down on some paper that you desire zest and you are open to any positive changes this may bring. Burn the paper and rub the ashes on the soles of your most used shoes. Wear them as much as possible for 10 days. Repeat if required.

Zoo: To receive animal guidance, go to a zoo and walk around. Look at as many animals as possible. Choose one that you really like and that you feel close to. From now on, whenever you desire guidance, you can go and 'talk' to your animal guide. Allow intuitive feelings to surface.

May the Gods walk with you and bless your path.

INDEX

abundance, 61
acceptance, 58, 74
affirmations, 25, 44, 48, 50–2, 107–8
ambitions, 90
athletic visualization, 85
attitude, 57

blocks, 54
blue paper, 31

candle meditation, 31
career, 88–95
cat stretch, 31
change, 21
colour, 112

day dreaming, 38
deep breathing, 29
diet, 82
divination, 109, 112

evolution, 102

fairy tales, 113
flowing, 53
forest, 40
fortune cards, 109

giving, 62
goddesses, 68
gods, 68

happiness, 98–9
health/healing, 81–7, 115, 116
hearing, 35
higher wills, 60
hobbies, 91

identity, 20
intent, 10
intuitive vibing, 118

Krishnamurti, 124

life, 102
love, 62, 96, 98

magic, 12
meditation, 60, 101
modern spells, 123
money, 73–80
music, 111

nature, 61
negativity, 8
New Age, 14

omens, 120
opening up, 36

passion, 42
pathworking, 38
patterns, 20
positivity, 8
preparation, 27
protection, 11
psychic attack, 106

reality, 22
receptive visualization, 100
relationships, 65–71
relaxation, 27, 28, 30
repression, 19
ritualizing, 118, 119

sea, 39

secret forces, 67
senses, 34
setting goals, 44–6
sex, 71–3
sight, 36
smell, 35
smoking, 87
space travel, 42
spirituality, 59, 100

talismans, 117
taste, 35
techniques, 101, 103
therapies, 13
thought, 8, 17, 18
tithing, 79
touch, 34

universal affirmations, 47

virtue, 11
visualization, 9, 12, 21–4, 44

white light, 84
will, 10
work, 88–95

X-factor, 18